Our Home in the Valley

The Centennial Celebration of the Daily News

Acknowledgments

THE LOS ANGELES DAILY NEWS AND THE SAN FERNANDO VALLEY HAVE grown up together, celebrating the good and weathering the bad. Their century-long journey is chronicled in Our Home in the Valley, a collaboration between the newspaper and the community that offers a glimpse of our ordinary and extraordinary times.

The book would not have been possible without the countless editors, reporters and photographers who have worked for the newspaper since its birth in 1911. Their talent, persistence and dedication have kept generations of readers in touch with their neighbors and civic leaders. Special thanks to the hundreds of young men and women who delivered the newspaper through the years. Readers often let us know that as youngsters, they delivered what was then affectionately called "The Green Sheet."

Thank you, too, to the newsmakers themselves and to the residents of the valleys we serve. Through their vision and hard work, the region has evolved into a vibrant and dynamic community that nearly 2 million people call home.

We received generous help from the staffs and archives of the following organizations: the Calabasas Historical Society, California State University Northridge, the San Fernando Valley Historical Society, Canoga-Owensmouth Historical Society and El Pueblo de Los Angeles Historical Monument.

Guy Weddington McCreary graciously granted us access to the extensive offerings in The Weddington Family Collection. The Herbert W. Allen Co., Malibu Creek Docents, Museum of the San Fernando Valley and the Valley Industry and Commerce Association also were outstanding resources.

In addition, more than three dozen residents contributed personal photographs at scanning sessions held throughout the region, including the West Valley Regional and Sherman Oaks branches of the Los Angeles Public Library.

Our thanks also go to employees of the Daily News who worked on this project: Dean Musgrove and Shane Kidder of the Photo Department and librarian Miriam Velasquez. Correspondents Kelly Corrigan and Andrea Hescheles were instrumental in combing 100 years worth of microfilmed archives for the historical material that made this book possible.

Special recognition to Editor Barbara Jones for her dedication in overseeing our year-long centennial research project and in editing much of this book.

Most of all, we want to thank all of the readers whose relationship with the newspaper over the last century has helped us thrive and serve the Valley we love to call home.

Jack D. Klunder
President & Publisher
Los Angeles Daily News

Carolina Garcia
Executive Editor
Los Angeles Daily News

LEFT: Los Angeles Daily News employees gather outside their Woodland Hills office, August 2011

Published by Pediment Publishing, a division of The Pediment Group, Inc. www.pediment.com Printed in Canada

4

Table of Contents

The Early Years

Indigenous peoples known as the Chumash, Tataviam and Fernandeño tribes of Indians were among the first residents of what is now the San Fernando Valley. They farmed the land for more than 6,000 years before the arrival of Spanish explorer Gaspar de Portola on Aug. 5, 1769. Father Juan Crespi, part of the expedition establishing a northward route from Mexico, described in his diary how he stood atop a ridge overlooking a "very pleasant and spacious valley." Noting that the hills and valleys were covered with walnut and live oak trees, Crespi named the plain Santa Catalina de Bononia de Los Encinos.

In the ensuing years, Franciscan missionaries converting the region's Indians to Christianity established the Mission San Fernando Rey de Espana, named for the king of Spain. The Indians were treated as slaves under the missionary system, which was disbanded after Mexico achieved its independence from Spain in 1821. Mexican officials established a system of land grants that spurred the settlement of Southern California.

The first stagecoach stopped at the top of the San Fernando Pass in December 1854, and the Santa Susana Pass was cut through in 1860 so the Overland Mail Co. could deliver the mail. The linking of the eastward and westward stretches of the overland railroad in May 1869 signaled the beginning of a land boom in the Valley and the real jumping-off point of its history.

Two months later, cash-poor Mexican Governor Pio Pico sold the southern half of the Valley for $115,000 to Isaac Lankershim, a grain farmer and member of the San Fernando Homestead Association. In 1872, Senator Charles Maclay bought the 56,000 acres in the northern half of the Valley for $117,500 and laid out the town of San Fernando. Hoping to draw settlers to the new community, agents met the trains and offered free barbecue lunches and tours of the acreage for sale. Town lots started at $50, farm lots at just $5.

By the late 1970s, Lankershim's wheat farm was flourishing. He acquired a partner, Isaac Newton Van Nuys, to oversee his farm while he began selling off some of his property in 40-acre ranchettes.

Trade centers were established in the 1880s as adventuresome settlers ventured to the Valley. George Porter sold land that later becomes Mission Hills. The 20,000-acre Maclay Colony became Sylmar. Tennessee speculator Jonette Allen founded Pacoima. Toluca was settled north of the Cahuenga Pass, eventually becoming Lankershim and, later, North Hollywood. By the end of the 1900s, motorcars appeared on roads crisscrossing the fertile farms and lush orchards that were growing as far as the eye could see.

OPPOSITE: An engineer and a passenger suffer minor injuries when a westbound Southern Pacific train derails shortly after leaving the Van Nuys Station, November 9, 1911.
Courtesy San Fernando Valley Historical Society

ABOVE: First Weddington ranch house at what is now the corner of Lankershim Boulevard and Weddington Street. North Hollywood was known as Toluca in 1894 when this picture was taken.
Courtesy The Weddington Family Collection

RIGHT TOP: San Fernando Mission in the late 1800s. Courtesy San Fernando Valley Historical Society

RIGHT BOTTOM: Wilson C. Weddington, appointed by President Grover Cleveland as postmaster of Toluca-Lankershim, is pictured in 1893 with Mary Weddington on the porch of their home, which also served as the local post office. Pictured in the buggies are Fred Weddington, left, and Guy Weddington.
Courtesy The Weddington Family Collection

ABOVE: A group of men club jackrabbits to death as the animals were destroying the crops in Lankershim.
Courtesy The Weddington Family Collection

LEFT: Businesses line San Fernando Road in Burbank, circa 1910.
Courtesy Daily News Archives

ABOVE: The Burbank Villa hotel opens on Olive Street in Burbank in 1887. It is later known as the Santa Rosa Hotel. Courtesy San Fernando Valley Historical Society

LEFT: A patch of pumpkins, fondly nicknamed 'Lankershim oranges' in the early 1900s. Courtesy The Weddington Family Collection

BELOW: W.H. Andrews, superintendent of the Lankershim Ranch Land and Water Co., oversees the clearing of land in the East Valley and Burbank for fruit orchards. Courtesy The Weddington Family Collection

ABOVE: Southern Pacific Engine 1677, known as the 'Toluca Flyer,' at the Lankershim Station, circa 1900. Courtesy Daily News Archives

ABOVE: Ladies Aid Society, circa 1910. Among those known are Margaret Sherman and Margaret Rodgers. Courtesy San Fernando Valley Historical Society

RIGHT TOP: Weddington Bros. General Merchandise Store on Chandler Boulevard, across from the train depot. Milo Weddington is seen at far left, Fred Weddington is in the car. Pioneer Store and Post Office are also seen. Courtesy The Weddington Family Collection

RIGHT BOTTOM: The Rooksby and Nelson families on an outing, circa 1910. The participants include, from left, Ed Rooksby, Marian Rooksby, Emma Ray Nelson and Mrs. Register.
Courtesy Canoga-Owensmouth Historical Society

BELOW: San Fernando Union High School, 1908.
Courtesy San Fernando Valley Historical Society

LEFT: Frieburg family at Toluca Lake enjoying their watermelon, circa 1908.
Courtesy Daily News Archives

BOTTOM LEFT: First picnic gathering at Griffith Park (at the old ostrich farm) for members of the Lankershim community and Sunday school class of the Methodist church, circa 1909. Courtesy The Weddington Family Collection

BOTTOM MIDDLE: The Davis family decked out in their tennis attire. The family came in 1895 and brought with them the sport of tennis all the way from Europe. From left, back row, are Hammond Davis, lawyer and owner of a glassworks shop in Italy; Euda Davis, Fred Weddington, Vick Davis. Second row are Anne Davis, Jinx, Marjorie Davis, Sky Weddington. Front row are unknown, Barbara Davis, Rina Davis and William Davis.
Courtesy The Weddington Family Collection

BOTTOM RIGHT: Construction of the Van Norman Reservoir (now called the Los Angeles Reservoir) in the North San Fernando Valley, circa 1913.
Courtesy San Fernando Valley Historical Society

ABOVE: Bruno Praster, second from right, establishes the first pool hall in San Fernando. Roy York stands to his right. Courtesy San Fernando Valley Historical Society

ABOVE: Henry Hollye Blacksmith shop located in San Fernando, circa 1910.
Courtesy San Fernando Valley Historical Society

ABOVE LEFT: T.W. Herron's meat market and grocery, located on the northwest corner of Magnolia and Lankershim boulevards, circa 1910.
Courtesy The Weddington Family Collection

LEFT: Inventor Joseph Fawkes built this prototype of an aerial monorail he hoped would carry passengers from Burbank to Los Angeles in 10 minutes. The trolley he calls the 'Aerial Swallow' becomes known as 'Fawkes Folly' after making a single, failed run on his Burbank ranch in 1907. Courtesy Daily News Archives

1911-1919

The impending birth of Van Nuys was heralded by a flood of real estate ads trumpeting "the largest opportunity on the entire Pacific Coast today." That lure of cheap land, along with the promise of a free barbecue, drew more than 10,000 people to an auction on February 22, 1911. Standing in a dusty field in the San Fernando Valley, buyers paid $350 for residential lots and $660 for business lots — a down payment on a place in "the town that was started right."

The town's namesake, Isaac Van Nuys, envisioned it as the civic and financial heart of a vast network of communities and business districts. In recording the largest subdivision in Los Angeles County, he included plans to develop three "wonder towns" — Van Nuys, Marian (now Reseda) and Owensmouth (now Canoga Park) — all linked by a system of highways and street cars.

Key to his plan was water, which was on its way from the Owens Valley via the Los Angeles Aqueduct. It flowed down the Sylmar spillway on November 5,

1913, destined for the growing city of Los Angeles. In 1915, San Fernando Valley residents voted overwhelmingly to annex to Los Angeles in order to have access to the municipal water supply.

By that time, Van Nuys and the surrounding towns were booming. Sherman Way (later renamed Van Nuys Boulevard) boasted 14 miles of roses, palms and five-light electroliers. Civic leaders organized a volunteer fire company and built a grammar school and a high school – "the pride of every citizen." The Johnston and Murray Harris organ companies announced plans to build factories in the Valley. Modern canneries opened to process the bountiful crops harvested by the region's growers and farmers. Despite the building boom, there were not enough homes, rooming houses and apartments to meet the demand, and those wanting to move to the Valley faced a "house famine."

With the entrance of the United States into World War I in April 1917, residents found their interests

diverted from the issues at home to those of draft registration, war bonds sales, sugar rationing and Red Cross drives. Local families shared with readers of The Van Nuys News the letters from husbands and sons fighting in Germany and France. "We remember the beauties of San Fernando Valley — the balmy winters and cool summers, the flowers and sunshine, the eternal greenness of orchards. We think often of the good things in life and the friends that were ours," reads a letter written by five local soldiers stationed together in France.

To the joy of their families, the boys who fought in the Great War began returning home in 1919, and the Van Nuys News again focused on local issues. National news occasionally crept onto the front page, such as the ratification of the 18th Amendment that mandated Prohibition. However, the passage of the 19th Amendment, giving women the right to vote, warranted nary a mention.

— *Barbara Jones*

OPPOSITE: William Boyd (aka Hopalong Cassidy) and an unknown starlet filming a movie at the home of Fredrick Blanchard. Courtesy Pamela Lundquist

Early On, Paper Acted as Booster

By Andrea Hescheles
Daily News Correspondent

THE TYPE IS SMALL, THE WRITING FLORID, THE PHOTOS FEW and far between.

Yet it's easy to envision life in the burgeoning San Fernando Valley from the news stories, announcements, gossip and even the advertisements published in the early years of The Van Nuys Call and its successor, The Van Nuys News.

"The ladies of Van Nuys are invited to come with sewing to the home of Miss Hazel Harding next Saturday evening," reads one of the "local notes" pub-lished on the front page of the paper's inaugural issue.

"E.J. Grobe and wife and Mrs. A.M. Harrison were the guests of Mr. Edinger to an automobile ride to Hollywood last Monday," reads another.

While much of that first issue was devoted to the type of gossip usually shared over a backyard fence, some of the tidbits hinted at the explosive growth of the community.

"Hugh Cass, district representative of Union Hardware & Metal Co., was in Van Nuys last Tuesday and after taking a large order from Andrew, the hardware man, said that in all of his travels, Van Nuys headed the list of suit-able locations, elegant homes and big hardware orders."

The Van Nuys Call was founded Oct. 13, 1911, by E.R. Elkins, some eight months after the founding of the town named for homesteader Isaac Van Nuys.

The first issue of the paper was published Nov. 3, 1911, with advertisements for well-drillers, building contractors and plumbers lining each side of the front page. Inside, the eight-page section carried an eclectic mix of news, jokes, fashion tips — hats covered in fancy feathers were all the rage — and even a short story or two.

Inexplicably, the issue was reproduced verbatim the following week.

On Nov. 24, 1911, the paper published for the first time as The Van Nuys News, whose new owner, Frank Keffer, made clear his plans to serve as a booster for the area. "For the Substantial Development of Our Town and Valley," it says on the left of the nameplate.

Keffer, a newspaper man from Pennsylvania, eliminated advertising from the front page to make room for news, which now included photos and images. Voters weighing a bond issue to build a $50,000 school were treated to a rendering of the project, rather than having to imagine it for themselves. (The bond was approved 80-0.)

As the News, the eight-page broadsheet focused heavily on local news, with stories of state, national and international interest mixed in. On March 15, 1912, for instance, the front page notes the discovery of the South Pole, the doubling of farm values in

LEFT TOP: San Fernando Baseball Team, 1911. Included in the group are Edward D. Lyon, Albert Garcia, Fred L. Nemback, Fred Candelot, Frank Holliday, Jim Jenifer, Charles Niblock, Clayton Troxel, Frank Pico, Raul Candelot and William Miller. Courtesy San Fernando Valley Historical Society

LEFT BOTTOM: Railroad workers in San Fernando Valley, circa 1911. Courtesy El Pueblo de Los Angeles Historical Monument

California, the construction of the Van Nuys Presbyterian Church and the dislocated thumb suffered by Roy Butterfield, a messenger for Wells Fargo Express.

Indeed, there was no event too small to warrant a mention in the paper: the new hitching post erected by H.S. Trotter in front of his Sherman Way grocery store; the names of all 42 members who attended a Parent Teacher Association meeting; and the guests at Hallie Huffaker's 16th birthday party.

Although routinely written in a passive voice — and never carrying a byline — the stories managed to capture the excitement and potential of the landmark events shaping the Valley.

A story trumpeting the December 1911 launch of a street-car route between Van Nuys and Los Angeles declares: "No doubt it will be the greatest event to be celebrated in all the valley's history for it means the establishment of a permanent and lasting blessing to all mankind. It has opened the door of opportunity to thousands of people who will flock to the valley, hungry for land and homes."

On May 3, 1912, the paper touted plans by Southern California Edison to start providing electricity to homes in Van Nuys at a cost of 7 cents per kilowatt hour. The same issue described plans to build a white-brick post office at Sherman Way and Virginia Street.

And on Oct. 18, 1912, the paper notes, "Within the next year, the San Fernando Valley, and especially that portion known as the Van Nuys-Lankershim lands, will have the finest system of improved highways to be found around Los Angeles."

Then, as now, Valley residents frequently found themselves at odds with those in Los Angeles, with issues such as annexation, development and the creation of the California Aqueduct spurring debate.

On Nov. 24, 1911, the News published the names of the 128 local residents objecting to "socialistic campaign misrepresentations in Los Angeles concerning ownership of San Fernando lands and its water supply" — an apparent reference to the syndicates secretly buying up Valley property as they negotiated for Owens River water.

Indeed, the issue of using Owens River water to irrigate the Valley's vast orchards and for its fledgling towns occupied space in nearly every edition of the weekly Van Nuys News.

"Concerted move for Owens Water," says a headline on May 10, 1912, topping a story that hints at efforts to annex to Los Angeles in order to secure water rights. "Do you want the Owens River water?" reads a bold headline printed four months later over a story advocating the project.

The Owens River water was needed not only to support the growth of the Valley but for irrigation of crops. With agriculture driving the Valley's economy, stories about rainfall, land values and crops frequently dominated the pages, including one in 1912 that boasted that Valley growers had planted the world's largest olive grove and sugar beet fields.

Throughout those early issues, there is unwavering support for the business, government and civic leaders whose actions were shaping the Valley. In fact, there is always the feeling that the paper is in partnership with the community and its residents.

A story published Aug. 20, 1912, about 18 months after the establishment of Van Nuys is headlined simply, "The town that was started right."

RIGHT: Workers lay track for Pacific Electric Railway's Red Car line, which arrives in the Valley in September 1911. The local routes are part of the 1,000-mile Southern California system, the world's longest. Courtesy CSUN, Ralph Samuels Collection

April 26, 1912

FIRST POPPY DAY IS CELEBRATED

The day was perfect and thousands of people from Los Angeles and nearby towns came to join in the festal occasion ... Never did the glorious fields of poppies which surround the town look prettier. A large Wilcox sight-seeing automobile was in attendance during the day, which met the incoming street cars and transported the visitors back and forth over the Boulevard from the golden fields, where they were at liberty to get out and pick as many of the flowers as they chose.

June 13, 1913

VALLEY WILL FURNISH GREAT HAY CROP

Reports from other parts of the state indicate that the San Fernando Valley will furnish the bulk of the hay crop this year ... This great hay crop is due to the natural moist condition of the soil, which is sub-irrigated and which made this valley for years the greatest hay field in the state.

ABOVE: Some 5,000 workers labor five years to complete the 233-mile-long Los Angeles Aqueduct. The guarantee of a steady water supply encourages the annexation of San Fernando Valley communities to Los Angeles.
Courtesy San Fernando Valley Historical Society

ABOVE LEFT: Water rushes through the Los Angeles Aqueduct on opening day, November 5, 1913. Engineer William Mulholland speaks at the dedication, saying, 'There it is. Take it.' Courtesy The Weddington Family Collection

ABOVE: San Fernando street scene, circa 1915.
Courtesy San Fernando Valley Historical Society

LEFT: Homesteaders Frank and Rob Straubinger haul hay in the wagon that carried the family from San Antonio to Calabasas, circa 1915.
Calabasas Historical Society, Straubinger Family Collection

July 31, 1914

PANAMA CANAL OPEN TO
TRAFFIC ON AUGUST 29

With confirmation from Washington that the Panama Canal would be open August 29, the harbor commission made the declaration that Los Angeles harbor is ready to care for the traffic and commerce of the world.

RIGHT: Andrews Hardware, the Bevis Bros. general store and Sutton Drug Store at Sylvan Street and Sherman Way (now Van Nuys Boulevard), 1916. Courtesy CSUN, Ralph Samuels Collection

LEFT TOP: Gilbert Stevenson and his family enjoy a traditional family picnic as Stevenson tended to his lemon ranch in San Fernando, 1918. Courtesy Tamara Celi

LEFT BOTTOM: An aerial view of Ventura Boulevard, circa 1917, Courtesy CSUN, Papers of the Reseda Chamber of Commerce

Nov. 8, 1918

JUST A TRIFLE PREMATURE

Along with the rest of the nation, Van Nuys has just begun to celebrate the unconditional surrender of Germany Thursday, when the official announcement from Washington that the armistice had not been signed called a halt ... The situation, however, is so full of promise that while the joy and jubilation may have been a little premature, it is only a matter of hours when we will be able to celebrate the official announcement.

LEFT: Calabasas Grammar School students on a school outing, 1918. Courtesy CSUN, Catherine Mulholland Collection

BELOW: Citrus-packing plants are a vital part of the Valley economy in the 1910s.
Courtesy San Fernando Valley Historical Society

June 8, 1917

VALLEY OFFERS MANY MEN FOR SERVICE

Without the least sign of disorder and with practically unanimous consent, 751 men between the ages of 21 and 31 were registered Tuesday for conscription in the eight city precincts of the San Fernando Valley. This number was far beyond the expectations of anyone who guessed on the number who would be registered.

Tarzana Sprang from Author's Land

Residents of the upscale suburb of Tarzana have undoubtedly heard the legend of how their community got its name. But the following story, published by the Van Nuys News on March 7, 1919, provides the details of the deal that placed the imprimatur of author Edgar Rice Burroughs on the Valley.

FAMOUS WRITER FOR SOUTH HILLS

TARZANA WILL BE THE NEW NAME OF MIRAFLORES, THE BEAUtiful improved country estate formerly owned by Gen. Harrison Gray Otis, in Van Nuys South Hills, which was purchased last week by Edward Rice Burroughs, famous American novelist, author of "Tarzan of the Apes," and other well known works.

Mr. Burroughs has been living in Los Angeles for several months, but the lure of the country life, where he can have seclusion of his writings and follow the pursuits of a California rancher, was the impelling motive for locating in the San Fernando Valley. He has taken possession of the estate and is now living there.

The estate, which comprises approximately 540 acres, lies along the south side of the Ventura boulevard, west of Encino Acres. Its center faces the newly paved Reseda avenue, and the property extends back to the sky line of the Santa Monica range of mountains.

A magnificent dwelling of the most modern hollow tile and concrete construction is built on a commanding knoll a half mile back from the highway,

---

RIGHT: Famous American novelist Edgar Rice Burroughs sits on his favorite horse, Colonel, at his Tarzana Ranch in 1928. Daily News Archives

from which one of the finest and most comprehensive views of the entire valley is had. This residence was built by General Otis and was occupied by him as a home at the time of his death.

Rare trees and shrubbery have been set out on a 15-acre plot around the house, which, when they attain their full growth, will make a veritable elysian

paradise of the place.

Acquired with the purchase were a large number of thoroughbred and registered goats, which the new owner will utilize on the hill lands and canyons of the estate.

Mr. Burroughs has also decided to engage extensively in the pig industry and is making plans for building up a herd of the finest Berkshire stock that he can secure.

The selection of the Van Nuys country for a home by Mr. Burroughs is another tribute to the attractiveness of this locality, for this noted author had all of Southern California to select from after a thorough search for a location.

As the News predicted early in the development of the Van Nuys tract, the south hills is rapidly developing into the greatest stock raising belt in the Southland. Already there are located along the Ventura boulevard the fine W.F. Holt Dairy and Stock Farm, the Adohr Stock Farm, owned by M.H. Adamson, and the celebrated Elliot-Brant Dairy and Stock Rancho.

Jan. 24, 1919

THE UNITED STATES WILL SOON BE A "DRY" NATION

The United States goes "dry." Within a few days over just one year from the time the prohibition amendment was submitted to the states, the measure was ratified. Nebraska was the 36th state to approve.

ABOVE: An aerial view of Tarzana Ranch, 1919. Author Edgar Rice Burroughs bought the estate from Gen. Harrison Gray Otis, founder of the Los Angeles Times. Courtesy Daily News Archives

April 11, 1919

VEGETABLE MARKET GROWS

The increasing production of vegetables, potatoes, spinach, lettuce, cabbage, melons, tomatoes and similar varieties of products on Van Nuys lands is rapidly bringing this community to the front as the real market basket of Southern California.

May 9, 1919

MANY SOLDIERS RETURN HOME

The Van Nuys boys are returning to their homes rapidly now from France, Belgium, Siberia and other parts of the war zone, where they gave heroic service to the government and brought honor and glory to themselves and their home town. Tales of the fighting and the wonderful experiences they have been through, keep the boys busy answering the hundred and one questions asked by their relatives and friends and in most cases they have brought with them relics from battlefields which prove of great interest.

Nov. 14, 1919

THRIFT FOR OUR PUBLIC SCHOOLS

Thrift is the latest subject to be added to the curriculum of the Los Angeles city schools. It is to be taught to the smallest tot in the primary grades and to the post-graduate student at the high school. State Superintendent of Public Instruction Wood has been made state director of thrift education by action of the treasury department.

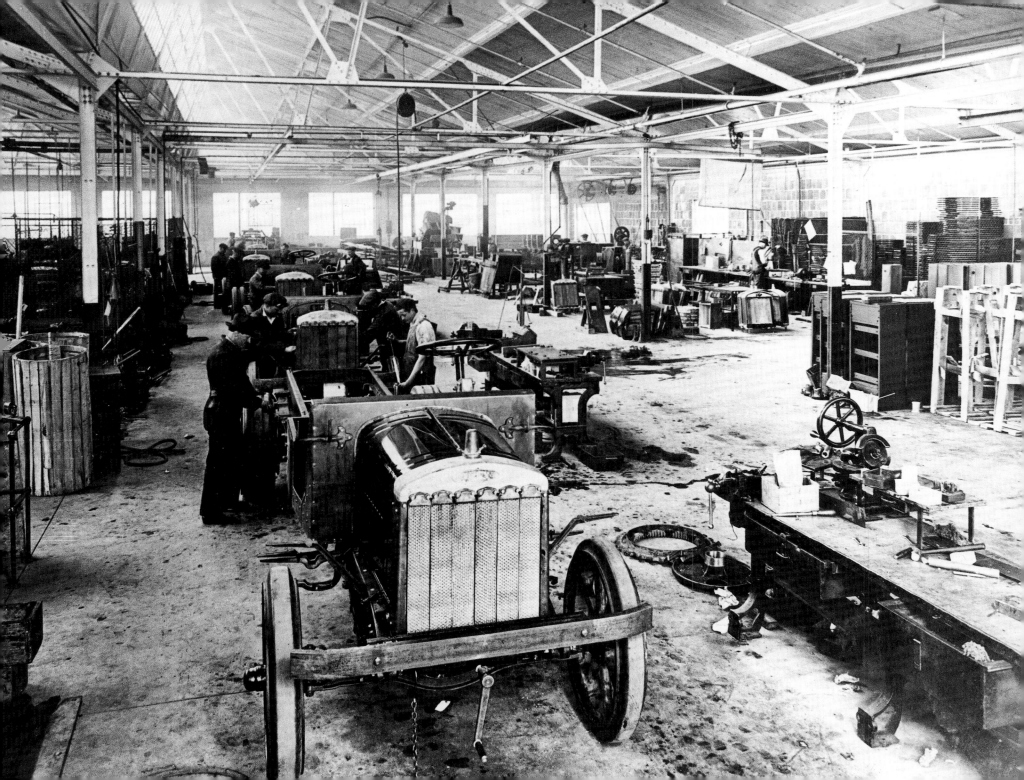

The 1920s

Van Nuys marked its 10th anniversary in 1921, a decade in which the area evolved from a tranquil farming community to a bustling township. However, the San Fernando Valley's agricultural roots continued to provide a strong base for industry. Canneries processed bumper crops of peaches and apricots, dairy and poultry farms flourished and food-industry giants like the H.J. Heintz Co. weighed a move to the region. The trade centers of Marian (Reseda), Tarzana and Encino were founded as people flocked to the area in search of prosperity.

Among those who recognized the Valley's potential was Walter Mendenhall, a veteran publisher from Missouri, who purchased a half-interest in The Van Nuys News in 1921. He and co-owner Frank Keffer soon added a second day of publication to accommodate the increase in advertising and local news as the Valley's population approached 25,000.

Progress and change were evident throughout the region. Roads were paved, power lines strung, streetcar lines extended. City engineer William Mulholland designed dams and drainage systems to protect the Valley from floods. The Valley police division expanded to 38 officers as more manpower was needed to handle a rash of traffic accidents and burglaries and to enforce the laws of Prohibition. Raids on bootleg stills included the discovery of a 3-gallon milk can attached to copper coils run by a moonshiner named Mrs. Dereois.

Although agriculture had long been the economic engine of the Valley, another industry was establishing a foothold. In 1927, a syndicate of 20 Los Angeles businessmen bought 500 acres in Van Nuys and created a Central Motion Pictures District to lure and promote entertainment companies. Filmmaker Mack Sennett's Famous Players was the first to announce plans to build a major studio in the district.

As hard as they worked, local residents valued their leisure time, too. They crowded Cornwell's Crystal Plunge – a public swimming pool – turned out in droves for Van Nuys' first-ever Halloween fest and flocked to the 820-seat Rivoli theater. Thousands made the trek to the inaugural Van Nuys Auto Show Beautiful, which featured vaudeville and instrumental entertainment. And it seemed that everyone had taken up the latest fad — crossword puzzles.

Overshadowing the decade's success, however, was the catastrophic collapse of the St. Francis Dam on March 12, 1928. Built to hold 12 billion gallons of water to supply the residents of Los Angeles, it had been filled to capacity just a week before the collapse. It unleashed a thundering wave 80 feet high that swept 54 miles through the Santa Clara River Valley — from what is now Santa Clarita to the Ventura coast — killing an estimated 600 people.

A catastrophe of a different sort — the stock market crash on Oct. 24, 1929 — took longer to have an impact on the Valley. Aviation had joined the agriculture, construction and entertainment industries in keeping the economy anchored as the 1930s dawned.

— *Barbara Jones*

OPPOSITE: Workers put the finishing touches on vehicles assembled at the Moreland Truck Co., which opened in 1920 at San Fernando Boulevard and Alameda Avenue in Burbank. Courtesy Daily News Archives

April 16, 1920

STRIKE HITS FARMERS HARD

The railroad strike has hit the farmers of the San Fernando valley a hard blow. Shipments of beans, lettuce, cabbage and other products produced here have been suspended and, as some of these articles are of perishable nature, the farmers face a big loss unless the strike is settled soon.

RIGHT: Employees at a Hammond Lumber Co. yard, circa 1920.
Courtesy Canoga-Owensmouth Historical Society

BELOW: Laborer Manuel Correia sits astride a cow in a Calabasas Public Market delivery truck. Correia lived on Peeler Ranch, which was known as Yearling Ranch when Ronald Reagan owned it from 1951-66. The property at Cornell Road and Mulholland Highway is now part of Malibu Creek State Park.
Courtesy Calabasas Historical Society

ABOVE: Bonner Fruit and Cannery Co. in Lankershim processes local produce and ships it across the U.S.
Courtesy The Weddington Family Collection

LEFT: The Samuels family poses in 1920 with carpenters who helped build their farmhouse at 8136 Louise Avenue, Northridge. Courtesy Dale Noll

FAR LEFT: The Whirlwinds basketball team, sponsored by Chapman & Morris Chevrolet, gathers for a group shot. Among those pictured are Bill Morris, standing second from left, and J. Everett Henderson, seated atop the car at right.
Courtesy San Fernando Valley Historical Society

BELOW: Owensmouth Gun Club, circa 1920.
Courtesy Canoga-Owensmouth Historical Society

Feb. 24, 1921

THOUSANDS TAKE PART IN BIG CELEBRATION

The tenth birthday of Van Nuys observed and commemorated by its citizens was an event that will dwell long in the memories of the thousands who took part. For its citizens, it brought pride and gratification. For the many visitors who were here, it brought wonder and admiration.

LEFT: Calabasas school boys take a moment to line up in the 1920s. From left are Percy Massen, Fred Tucker, Frank Cooper, Walt Penland, Joe Lee, Stanley Massen and Jerry Grant. Courtesy Calabasas Historical Society

OPPOSITE: Brand Boulevard in Glendale in the 1920s. Courtesy Daily News Archives

BELOW: Reseda Boulevard, south from Devonshire in the 1920s. Courtesy Daily News Archives

June 16, 1921

HIGHER SALARIES FOR LOS ANGELES TEACHERS

During the next school year, 1921-22, Los Angeles City School District, which includes the city schools and those of a number of the suburban cities, will expend $9,315,125 for teachers' salaries. Under the new budget announced by the board this week there will be a general salary increase which will aggregate $613,850. Van Nuys teachers will all share in this increase. The scale of salaries now ranges from $140 a month to $405. Elementary school teachers will receive approximately $30 more each month than at present; high school principals $40, and vice principals $20.

ABOVE: Arie Mason Carter, wearing a white skirt and hat, stands next to Fredrick Blanchard at a fund-raising event for the Hollywood Bowl. Courtesy Pamela Lundquist

June 1, 1922

HELP NEEDED TO HANDLE FRUIT

With the greatest fruit crop in the history of the Van Nuys community this season, the growers are confronted with a gigantic task of getting the peaches and apricots thinned and picked. The thinning time is here now and many orchards will have to be neglected on account of not being able to secure help to do the work.

Sept. 15, 1922

TARZANA - NEW TOWN TO BE ESTABLISHED

Following the announcement of the subdivision of the Miller property on Ventura Boulevard and Reseda Avenue and the Long Acres tract on Ventura boulevard opposite the Adohr Dairy, comes the announcement of the immediate subdivision of 100 acres of Tarzana Ranch, with 2,000 feet frontage on Ventura boulevard opposite Reseda Avenue, at the junction of which avenue with Ventura boulevard the new town of Tarzana is being established.

LEFT TOP: Southwest corner of San Fernando Road and South Brand Boulevard, 1923. Courtesy San Fernando Valley Historical Society

LEFT BOTTOM: Former Treasury Secretary William Gibbs McAdoo speaks at a rally at Bakman School in North Hollywood, 1923. Courtesy The Weddington Family Collection

ABOVE: View of Lankershim Boulevard about 13 miles from downtown Los Angeles in 1923. Courtesy San Fernando Valley Historical Society

RIGHT: Schoolchildren in North Hollywood, 1923.
Courtesy The Weddington Family Collection

OPPOSITE: The Encino Country Club opens in 1923, a year after the community is founded, at the southern terminus of Hayvenhurst Avenue. It gradually falls into disrepair and is known as the Valley's 'haunted house' by the time it is demolished in 1952. Courtesy Daily News Archives

Feb. 2, 1923

POPULATION OF VALLEY REACHES ABOUT 25,000

The total population of the San Fernando valley is 25,000 as estimated by the News from statistics of registrations and elections for 1922-1923.

RIGHT TOP: Owensmouth High School Football team, 1924. Courtesy Canoga-Owensmouth Historical Society

RIGHT BOTTOM: Sherman Way looking east, 1924. Courtesy Canoga-Owensmouth Historical Society

Jan. 15, 1924

VACCINATION FOR SMALLPOX

To combat in Van Nuys the mild epidemic of smallpox that is sweeping Los Angeles county and that has already touched this community through the twenty cases that have been discovered in the district, a vaccination station was established this morning by the health department near the grammar school.

Nov. 18, 1924

AUTO SPEEDERS NEWLY WARNED

Auto speeders on the Van Nuys highways and boulevards had better take warning anew, for the speeding laws in Los Angeles county and the city are being rigidly enforced and reckless drivers are being given serious penalties. Yesterday in Los Angeles more than 500 motorists were arrested and charged with speeding and reckless driving.

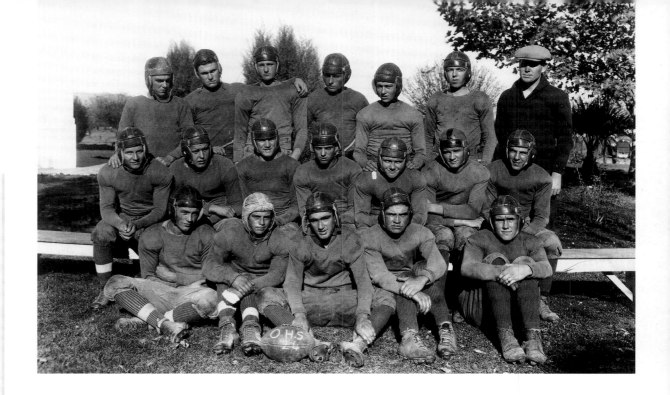

April 3, 1926

AN EXTENSIVE PAVING PROGRAM FOR VALLEY

A paving program of our 42 miles in the central portion of the valley is being carried on this year ... The longest of these projects will be Balboa Avenue ... It will be twelve and a half miles long and run from Ventura boulevard to San Fernando road.

ABOVE: Brothers Stanley and Loren Brown are pictured at the Tarzana farm owned by Elsa Rigg Brown and David Crane Brown, circa 1925. The Browns grow apricots and walnuts on their farm at 18718 Ventura Boulevard. Courtesy Melissa Brown Biderman

RIGHT: Owensmouth High School girls basketball team photo, 1926. Courtesy Canoga-Owensmouth Historical Society

BELOW: Retired Los Angeles Fire Chief Herbert W. Allen is pictured in 1927 in front of a volunteer fire station at 7224 Remmett Avenue in Owensmouth.

Courtesy Andrew Allen

Oct. 22, 1926

SLENDER GIRLS ARE TO BE MADE PLUMP BY DIET AT HIGH SCHOOL

In every school in the land, there are certain underweight girls who probably would be as plump as the rest of their classmates, if more attention were paid to their diet. The Van Nuys High School teachers are going to make an effort to solve the problem. An innovation will be a "mid-morning lunch" ... Starting next Tuesday all who are qualified for the lean class will go to the cafeteria porch where they will be served graham crackers and milk.

LEFT: View of Burbank looking east on Olive Street, 1927.
Courtesy Daily News Archives

BELOW: Van Nuys Boulevard at Delano Street looking north, 1927. Courtesy Maureen Lippert

March 22, 1927

BIG STUDIO DEAL INVOLVES FIVE HUNDRED ACRES

The most stupendous moving picture deal ever undertaken in the city of Los Angeles was nearing completion today with the purchase of 500 acres of choice valley land near Van Nuys to be developed for moving picture studio purposes, according to the reports. A syndicate of twenty Los Angeles businessmen, many of them the most prominent business leaders of the city has virtually completed the purchase of the 500-acre block fronting on Pacoima avenue and extending from Chandler boulevard to Ventura boulevard.

St. Francis Dam Collapses

By Kelly Corrigan
Daily News Correspondent

THE ST. FRANCIS DAM COLLAPSED IN THE LAST FEW MINUTES of March 12, 1928, unleashing a towering wall of water that killed as many as 600 people.

The tragedy stands more than 80 years later as the second-deadliest disaster in California history, with only the 1906 San Francisco Earthquake claiming more lives.

The extent of the catastrophe was not yet realized when The Van Nuys News published a story on March 13 that carried the banner headline, "Scores die in flood disaster." However, the dramatic prose

depicted the calamity that occurred just a few miles north of the San Fernando Valley:

"With a thundering, deafening roar that rocked San Francisquito Canyon to its very depths and then echoed and re-echoed up through the higher levels, St. Francis Dam, the pride of the Los Angeles aqueduct system, gave way at 1 a.m. today, a wall of water 40 feet high swept down the canyon carrying all before it — and death stalked in its wake."

Later estimates put the wave as high as 80 feet as it swept 54 miles through the Santa Clara River Valley — from what is now Santa Clarita to the Ventura coast — an area that was home to roughly 20,000 people.

Some residents downstream were lucky enough to receive a warning and were able to evacuate in time. Hundreds of others — estimates range from 470 to 600 — were drowned or swept away, their bodies never found.

Subsequent stories told of efforts to find victims, with local Boy Scouts and members of the Van Nuys High School ROTC fanning out in the flooded fields

around Fillmore in the search for bodies.

The dam was built between 1924 and 1926 along a stretch of the aqueduct, creating a three-mile-long reservoir holding 12 billion gallons of water to supply the residents of Los Angeles.

It had been filled to capacity just a week before the collapse, and there were reports that water was leaking from cracks in the structure. William Mulholland, the self-taught civil engineer who had designed the aqueduct as well as the dam, inspected the dam and determined it was sound.

However, Frank Rock, a Santa Clarita historian who has extensively studied the disaster, believes there were significant problems with the dam.

The first, he said, was that the dam was likely built on the site of an ancient landslide, creating an unstable foundation for the massive structure.

Equally critical was Mulholland's decision, made when the dam was halfway complete, to raise its height by 10 feet without making significant changes to the base.

"The slide was the one thing that brought it down," Rock said, "but it was brewing not to be a very good dam."

The flood effectively finished Mulholland's career. He carried the blame and retired at the year's end, a story that was carried by The Van Nuys News on Dec. 7, 1928.

"He did some consulting work," Rock said, "but he was damaged after that completely."

ABOVE: View of the lettuce fields and workers on the southwest corner of Sepulveda Boulevard and Victory Boulevard in Van Nuys, 1928. The land was farmed by Wallace Dickey.
Courtesy Don L. Brown and Syd R. Brown II

OPPOSITE: The St. Francis Dam had been filled to capacity just a week before it collapsed, causing death and destruction downstream. The dam, built between 1924 and 1926 along a stretch of the aqueduct, held 12 billion gallons of water.
Courtesy Santa Clarita Historical Society

May 4, 1928

GIRL DROPS IN PLANE TO CURE DEAFNESS

Climbing by airplane to an altitude of 14,500 feet in the air and dropping ten thousand feet in ten drops of a thousand feet each, was the thrilling experience of little 3-year-old Daisy Jackson, of Los Angeles as the passenger of honor in one of those interesting experiments being carried on in the aviation world as a cure for deafness... There was no immediate evidence as to the effect of the experiment, as it is understood that it requires from two to three days before the results fully develop.

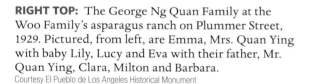

RIGHT TOP: The George Ng Quan Family at the Woo Family's asparagus ranch on Plummer Street, 1929. Pictured, from left, are Emma, Mrs. Quan Ying with baby Lily, Lucy and Eva with their father, Mr. Quan Ying, Clara, Milton and Barbara.
Courtesy El Pueblo de Los Angeles Historical Monument

RIGHT BOTTOM: San Fernando Junior Cosmos in 1929, from left, Mrs. Carroll Nare, Mrs. Quentin Johnson, Mrs. Jack Hood and Mrs. Alan Rueff, president. The group is the predecessor of the San Fernando Junior F's Club.
Courtesy San Fernando Valley Historical Society

OPPOSITE: Aviation pioneers Elinor Smith, 17, and Bobbi Trout, 23, at Van Nuys Airport on Nov. 27, 1929, prior to setting a new woman's endurance record of 42 hours in their Sunbeam biplane.
Courtesy Daily News Archives

ABOVE: Cars headed north on Lankershim in the 1920s. Courtesy The Weddington Family Collection

March 5, 1929

HUNDREDS AT INAUGURATION DAY EVENT, SHERMAN OAKS

Several hundred residents of Cahuenga Park and Sherman Oaks gathered at the Community auditorium last night where an excellent Presidential Inauguration Day program was given for the two-fold purpose of honoring President Hoover and reviewing the progress made in the development of the twin communities.

March 19, 1929

HOME BUILDING IS LEADING ACTIVITY

The erection of new homes continues to be the major activity throughout the Valley. Work on a score of new dwellings in the Van Nuys area has been started following the granting of permits last week by the local office of the building department.

Nov. 22, 1929

MISS EARHART BREAKS WORLD RECORD

Amelia Earhart, famous feminine pilot, broke the world's speed record for women here yesterday, when she drove her Lockheed-Vega monoplane at 185 miles per hour over a prescribed course at Metropolitan airport. Miss Earhart drove the cabin plane, powered by a 425-horsepower Wasp motor at well over 180 miles per hour according to the airspeed indicator, but owing to the failure of the timing piece being used by Joe Nikrent, official of the National Aeronautic association, the flight cannot be recorded as official. Another attempt is to be made later.

LEFT: Amelia Earhart poses in front of her airplane.
Courtesy The Weddington Family Collection

ENCINO STORE

GROCERIES · FOUNTAIN

The 1930s

MOMENTUM FROM THE SUCCESSFUL AGRICULTURE, AVIATION and entertainment industries buoyed the San Fernando Valley as it entered the 1930s. Seemingly untouched by the stock market crash in October 1929, residents in 1930 celebrated the opening of United Airport in Burbank, a post office in Tarzana and Valley Hospital, a J.C. Penney store and a miniature golf course in Van Nuys.

However, the prosperity and optimism that marked the first two decades of Van Nuys' existence evaporated in 1931 and 1932 as the region — like the rest of the country – fell victim to the Great Depression. Banks failed, businesses closed and growers slashed farmworkers' wages. With audiences in soup lines instead of movie theaters, the entertainment industry struggled to survive. Refugees fleeing the Dust Bowl in the Midwest joined local residents in unemployment lines.

Yet communities joined to aid struggling neighbors. The San Fernando Valley was one of several districts in California where self-help cooperatives help residents find work. And some of the region's greatest successes resulted from federal loans that put tens of thousands of Los Angeles County residents to work building parks, freeways and other public works projects.

The mid-1930s brought hints that the grim days were ending. Housing developers returned to the Valley, businesses opened and welfare rolls shrank as people went back to work.

Movie studios entered their "golden age," an era when they would produce some of Hollywood's classic movies and most-beloved stars. Scores of these celebrities made their home in the Valley, acquiring ranches, small farms and country estates in the shadow of Hollywood studios.

As their worries about the economy eased, residents could again focus on civic and neighborhood issues. Chief among them were regulating bars and beer halls that had sprung up following the end of Prohibition. There were also whispers about a growing communist threat and meetings to discuss a strategy for squelching agitators.

By the end of the decade, the newly opened Van Nuys City Hall was abuzz with activity, and the region's roadways were again crowded with motorists. With its investment in neighborhoods and industry, the Valley led the country in per-capita construction spending, evidence that a new building boom was well under way.

— *Barbara Jones*

OPPOSITE: The Encino Store and Post Office opens in April 1938. Among those pictured are actors Don Ameche, Phil Harris and Edward Everett Horton, and prominent landowner Peter Amestoy. Al Jolson, the honorary mayor of Encino, is at the center, holding the white hat. Courtesy Calabasas Historical Society

March 7, 1930

DIAL PHONES CUT IN AT OWENSMOUTH

Owensmouth's new dial telephone system will be cut into service at seven o'clock Friday morning, March 14. According to C.C. Campbell, manager of The Pacific Telephone and Telegraph company, the new system under construction since October represents an expenditure of more than $65,000 and is the most modern type now in use ... About 300 telephones will be converted from the naval to the dial at the time of the cultivar.

ABOVE LEFT: Calabasas school district children in the 1930s. Courtesy Calabasas Historical Society

ABOVE RIGHT: Inside an orange-packing house, circa 1930. Courtesy San Fernando Valley Historical Society

LEFT: Hazeltine Packing Company, located between San Fernando Road and the tracks, west of Maclay, circa 1930. Courtesy San Fernando Valley Historical Society

June 27, 1930

1600 "EXTRA" PLAYERS IN WAR FILM PRODUCTION ON VALLEY RKO RANCH

Sixteen-hundred "extra" players were made happy yesterday by being selected for work in Radio Pictures' all-talking wartime comedy, "Half Shot at Sunrise," production of which is scheduled to start next week at the RKO ranch near Encino, according to plans revealed today at the studio.

LEFT: Aviation companies and support industries such as Union Gasoline, Lippiatt and Bach Aircraft Company began thriving at Van Nuys Airport in the 1930s. Courtesy Daily News Archives

BELOW LEFT: The Van Nuys Chamber of Commerce building in the 1930s. It later houses the Daily News. Courtesy CSUN, Ralph Samuels Collection

BELOW RIGHT: Two members of the first Glendale Fire Department are pictured with the department's biplane, circa 1930. Courtesy Daily News Archives

ABOVE: Poultry became the dominant industry in the 1920s and 1930s in the North Hollywood area. The area was known as the 'Home of the Hen.'
Courtesy The Weddington Family Collection

RIGHT: Bing Crosby on his boat fishing in the 1930s. He lived on Camarillo Street in Toluca Lake.
Courtesy The Weddington Family Collection

BELOW: Interior of Lyons Drug Store, circa 1930. At right stands Mark Lyon, brother-in-law of Howard Pearson and nephew of Charlie Lyon, who started the store.
Courtesy CSUN, Catherine Mulholland Collection

ABOVE: Crowds gather for the dedication of United Airport in Burbank in May 1930. For more than a decade, it was the largest commercial airport in Southern California. After several name changes, the facility was dedicated in 2003 as Bob Hope Airport in honor of the famed comedian.

Jan. 20, 1931

LOCAL DAIRYMEN FACING SERIOUS SITUATION AS DEPRESSION HITS MARKET

Because the price of butterfat has fallen below the cost of production, dairymen in the San Joaquin and Imperial Valley are attempting to change from butter and cream production and send market milk into Los Angeles.

March 10, 1932

LEGION EMPLOYMENT DRIVE MAKING GREATER STRIDES

Steadily marching forward in the "war against depression" the forces of the American Legion in cooperation with other national agencies are making greater strides toward placing one million idle workers in jobs. The employment campaign is gathering momentum and recording more and more new jobs for the unemployed each day.

ABOVE: Fire Station 72, 'B' shift. Captain E.S. Snively, and firemen, E.H. Newmyer, R.J. McLaughlin, and J.L. Stringer. *Courtesy Canoga-Owensmouth Historical Society*

ABOVE LEFT: Headquarters of the North Hollywood Chamber of Commerce in the 1930s. Also known as the relief headquarters throughout the Great Depression. *Courtesy The Weddington Family Collection*

LEFT: Henrietta Vasquez in the 1930s. *Courtesy Lorrie Lopez Carillo*

April 6, 1933

BEER TO FOAM OVER COUNTY TOMORROW

Beer will foam over approximately four-fifths of Los Angeles county Friday when national legislation turns on the spigot closed for 13 years, it was indicated as city councils in most of the municipalities hurried to pass emergency liquor laws.

LEFT: Amelia Earhart and three unidentified men in front of a Lockheed hangar in 1932. Courtesy CSUN

BELOW LEFT: View of Daic Garage after a snowfall on Calabasas Road, 1932. Courtesy Calabasas Historical Society

BELOW RIGHT: Floats in the Fiesta Parade coming down San Fernando Road, 1930s.
Courtesy San Fernando Valley Historical Society

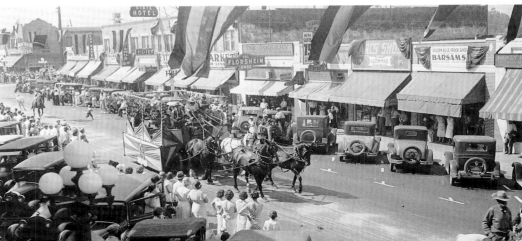

April 16, 1934

ONE OF SIX PERSONS ON CHARITY

Cash doles to unemployed on the county charity rolls this week loomed as a substitute for the percent direct relief, under which grocery orders, small cash supplement and milk orders are issued and rent and public utility bills are paid by the county. The number of families dependent on the county charity stood at 93,301 or nearly 375,000 persons, more than one out of every six persons in the county.

May 10, 1934

PENALTY KILLS LICENSE IDEA FOR BICYCLES

A proposal to require bicycles to have a license similar to the motor vehicle tax, at a fee of 50 cents a year, was virtually killed in the City Council this week.

July 19, 1934

4876 AUTOMOBILES ENTER VAN NUYS INTERSECTION IN SIX HOURS

Wednesday is normally a quiet day in the business district of Van Nuys, but a traffic check made yesterday by the Traffic Bureau of the Los Angeles Police department revealed that a total of 4,876 automobiles entered the intersection of Van Nuys boulevard and Sylvan street, between the hours of 7:30 and 10:30 a.m. and 3:00 and 6:00 p.m.

ABOVE: Students at Topeka Drive Elementary in Northridge portray Maid Marian and Robin Hood and his Merry Men during a May Day celebration, circa 1935. Courtesy Melissa Brown Biderman

ABOVE LEFT: The San Fernando Super Market team from the San Fernando Athletic Club, 1934. Courtesy San Fernando Valley Historical Society

OPPOSITE: Encino Company 73 firefighters gather in front of a fire engine and the firehouse, circa 1935. Courtesy Daily News Archives

BELOW: Students from Las Virgenes School on an outing in Los Angeles. Courtesy Calabasas Historical Society

ABOVE: San Fernando Fiesta Parade, 1937. The Hazeltine Packing House and Killen Float won first prize. From left are Estella Lyon Maas, Irene Lyon Miranda, Josephine Soto, Ramona Lopez Asher, Vera Hunt, Lydia Real Pesquiera and Ignacio Pesquiera. Courtesy San Fernando Valley Historical Society

OPPOSITE: Van Nuys Boulevard looking south from Arminta just north of where the Southern Pacific coast line crosses Van Nuys Boulevard. Pacific Electric car 838 on its way to San Fernando in 1937. Pacific Electric ran down the middle of Van Nuys Boulevard from Chandler Boulevard to Parthenia Street.
Courtesy Robert Peppermuller and the Craig Rasmussen Collection

May 9, 1935

LOS ANGELES POPULATION HAS INCREASED 8.93 PER CENT SINCE 1930 CENSUS

The population of Los Angeles has shown an increase of 110,781, or 8.93 per cent, since the last census, according to a comprehensive county-wide estimate of population made recently by the Western Statistical Association of Los Angeles. According to this estimate the population of the City of Los Angeles amounted to 1,351,140 in January 1934 as compared with 1,238,048 as shown by the 1930 census.

June 24, 1935

MILK MEN WILL GET THAT EXTRA WINK OF SLEEP

Five thousand Los Angeles milk truck drivers won their fight for an ordinance to abolish pre-dawn delivery of milk throughout the city ... The measure provides that milk trucks stay off the city streets except between 8 a.m. and 7 p.m.

Aug. 13, 1936

SOLD PLAIN EARTH FOR FERTILIZER

A new racket - that of selling plain earth for fertilizer - was uncovered in the Valley yesterday as the result of an experience a property owner had with two men driving a truck, which he reported to police ... They were given a check for $6 in payment, but when the gardener arrived he told his employer that he had made no such arrangement and that the material that was supposed to be fertilizer was just ordinary soil.

Oct. 8, 1936

BUILD STABLES TO TRAIN BEST SADDLE HORSES

Some of Southern California's finest saddle stock will be trained in Van Nuys in the future as a result of negotiations closed yesterday when two well-known trainers formed a corporation known as Rancho Cortez and awarded a contract for the construction of modern stables at 13504 Hart Street ... Fifteen animals, one a descendant of the great Rex McDonald, will be housed in the stables as soon as they are finished, about November 1. The owners will train horses for fairs and circuses and also for bridle paths.

May 27, 1937

ANGULAR PARKING IS APPROVED

Angular parking of automobiles on Van Nuys boulevard in the business district of this city was approved this week by the Los Angeles Police Commission, and today white lines are being painted on the pavement in order that the maximum number of cars can be parked safely at the curbs.

RIGHT TOP: The entrance to Adohr Certified Farm, circa 1937. In the 1930s, the San Fernando Valley dairy produced more certified milk than any other farm in the country. Courtesy CSUN

RIGHT BOTTOM: Amelia Earhart receives a plane antenna at Bendix Aviation in Burbank, 1937. Courtesy The Weddington Family Collection

OPPOSITE: Sherman Way is awash after a series of heavy rainstorms causes widespread flooding. The Los Angeles Flood of 1938 kills an estimated 115 people and causes some $40 million in damage. Courtesy Canoga-Owensmouth Historical Society

ABOVE: Entire neighborhoods in the East Valley are isolated when Big Tujunga Wash and Los Angeles River flood in March 1938. Courtesy The Weddington Family Collection

OPPOSITE TOP: Flash floods damage Magnolia Boulevard near what is now Valley Village. Courtesy Louis Kleinau

OPPOSITE BOTTOM LEFT: An unidentified motorist is caught unaware by flash floods that swept through North Hollywood in March 1938. Courtesy The Weddington Family Collection

OPPOSITE BOTTOM RIGHT: This home is among the 5,600 structures destroyed by the 1938 flood.
Courtesy The Weddington Family Collection

Sept. 2, 1937

TOURISTS SPENDING
$27,240 AN HOUR IN SOUTHLAND

Spending their money at the rate of more than $27,240 an hour, tourists are visiting Southern California in greater numbers this summer than ever before. By the end of the summer season, if the present rate of pleasure travel is maintained, an all time record breaking total of 1,129,128 paying guests will have visited the Southland and will have spent approximately $119,631,112.

Clark Gable buys Walsh Encino Place

ANOTHER GLAMOROUS PERSON HAS BECOME A RESIDENT OF Encino ... with the announcement that Clark Gable, star of the motion picture world, has just purchased the estate of Raoul Walsh, famous director, where he plans his home. The property consists of 14 acres of highly developed and rare fruit. Many natural trees make a beautiful setting. The Connecticut type farm house of twelve rooms will be rearranged. The present barns will house several riding horses and the addition of a swimming pool will make what Mr. Gable calls "the place he has always hoped to own."

ABOVE: Clark Gable purchased the Encino estate of director Raoul Walsh in 1939, the year "Gone with the Wind" premiered. The land, full of fruit trees, included a 12-room farm house. Courtesy Daily News Archives

ABOVE RIGHT: Participating in a campaign to buy land for Orcutt Ranch are, from left, Dorothy House, Adelaide Armstrong and Alta Speer with Walter Hansen, manager of California Bank, 1939.
Courtesy Canoga-Owensmouth Historical Society

March 13, 1939

RABID DONKEY ATTACKS FOUR

Pandemonium reigned at a Van Nuys ranch for a few tense moments early Friday afternoon when a customary gentle male donkey went berserk and bit the owner and two employees of the ranch. Another employee received a painful scalp wound when hit by a club in the general melee to release one man's arm from the donkey's jaw. The crazed animal, tethered in a field, was believed to have been bitten by a rabid coyote that ranged down from the south hills.

July 20, 1939

MANY ENTRIES FOR DACHSHUND SHOW IN VALLEY SUNDAY

By all indications, the annual puppy show which the Dachshund Club of California will hold in Griffith Park at 1 o'clock on July 30, will be one of the largest ever held outside of New York ... If you own a Dachshund or if you like them or if you like dogs, or just if, Griffith Park on Sunday, July 30, will be a very interesting place.

LEFT: Employment line at Vega Airplane Company, circa 1939. Courtesy CSUN, Del Stelk Collection

BELOW: Lucy Fonseca (center) standing with two friends from her junior high. Courtesy Della Ortega

July 20, 1939

YOUNG WIFE TAKES LIFE WHILE HUSBAND TALKS TO NUDISTS

While her husband conversed on the telephone, Mrs. Dawn Noel, 19-year-old bride of a year of Herbert James Noel, 36-year-old orchestra leader, committed suicide Tuesday ... Noel told police Capt. Z.P. Magness that he was at the telephone, "bawling out" a friend about a nudist party over the week-end, at a nudist camp in the San Fernando Valley. He said his wife went into the bedroom and then he heard the death shot fired ... He said he could not explain her act.

The 1940s

THE 1940S STARTED OFF WITH RELIEF. THE GREAT DEPRESsion had ended, businesses were again prospering, and residents were living in idyllic neighborhoods in the vast open spaces north of Los Angeles. That world changed on Dec. 7, 1941, when the Japanese attack on Pearl Harbor launched the U.S. into World War II.

The war infiltrated all aspects of life in the San Fernando Valley. Men enlisted or reported to their draft boards, then went to fight in Europe and the Pacific. At home, residents rationed food, gasoline, tires and metal – materials vital to the war effort. Air-raid sirens were erected in the Valley, and blackout curtains went up in many homes. A 1,720-bed Army hospital was built at Victory and Balboa boulevards.

The Valley's burgeoning aviation industry quickly converted to defense work, with women assuming the role of "Rosie the Riveter" on the assembly lines. Bus service was expanded to ensure that defense workers could get to and from their jobs. And when the call went out to help solve the housing shortage for additional workers needed in the munitions plants, 300 Valley families offered to rent out a spare room.

America celebrated the surrender of Nazi Germany in May 1945 and of Japan three months later, bringing a joyous end to World War II. Once again, the Valley experienced a population boom as military veterans returned home seeking work and family life. By the end of the year, plans were in the works to build a General Motors factory and a general-aviation airport in Van Nuys. Construction also started on Pierce Agricultural School in Woodland Hills, although some worried that the sprawling neighborhoods springing up around the Valley would spell an end to the Valley's agricultural dominance.

By the end of the decade, in fact, nearly a half-million people lived in the Valley – completing its evolution from a suburban hideaway to a major population center.

— *Barbara Jones*

OPPOSITE: Bird's-eye view of San Fernando Valley. The LA river is seen in the background. Ventura Boulevard runs left to right in the middle. Courtesy The Weddington Family Collection

Sept. 12, 1940

FREE BUS TRANSPORTATION FOR VALLEY SCHOOL STUDENTS

Free bus transportation for elementary and high school students residing within the boundaries of the designated areas will be available beginning Sept. 16 with the opening of public schools, according to an announcement issued today ... Those ineligible for free bus transportation are post-graduate pupils of senior high schools, city college pupils and regular elementary and high school students living within the mileage limits.

Nov. 7, 1940

VALLEY VOTERS GIVE DEMOCRATIC CANDIDATES MAJORITIES

San Fernando Valley voters, in general with those of the nation, gave Franklin D. Roosevelt a substantial majority over the Republican candidate, Wendell L. Willkie, and was elected president of the United States for the third consecutive term. The vote was the heaviest ever recorded in this district. In the 76 precincts of the central and western parts of the Valley, a total of 20,636 ballets were cast for President, of these 11,765 were for Roosevelt and 8621 were for Willkie. The remaining 250 were divided among the other three parties.

RIGHT TOP: Aerial view of Granada Hills, 1940.
Courtesy San Fernando Valley Historical Society

RIGHT BOTTOM: Sherman Way, Canoga Park, 1940s. Courtesy Canoga-Owensmouth Historical Society

ABOVE: Group of men and women dressed in western wear for the Canoga Park Cavalcade, circa 1940s. Courtesy CSUN

LEFT: Lucille Ball and Desi Arnaz leave Our Lady of the Valley Catholic Church in Canoga Park in 1940. Courtesy Canoga-Owensmouth Historical Society

BELOW: Busy street scene in the early 1940s at the corner of Lankershim and Weddington in North Hollywood. Courtesy The Weddington Family Collection

Nov. 18, 1940

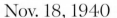

DOG SAVES MAN'S LAST SIX DOLLARS

Roy Merry's pet cocker spaniel was a hero in his own right's today. He saved a man's last six dollars. The dog retrieved the wallet containing the money, identification cards and a pawn ticket from the roadside after Arthur P. Erickson, laborer, residing at 1555 Ocean Ave., Santa Monica had been arrested in front of 15739 Ventura Blvd., on a charge of intoxication, police reports show. Carrying the purse in his mouth, the dog took it home and scratched on the door.

THIS IS TILLIE'S PLAYMATE "DINAH"

SHIRLEY TEMPLE'S GUERNSEY CALF 'TILLIE TEMPLE' of Tillamook

LEFT: Shirley Temple visits "Tillie," a Guernsey calf purchased for her in May 1935 by young fans in Tillamook County, Oregon. Adohr Farms in Encino keeps the calf for the popular child star. Courtesy CSUN

OPPOSITE: At right is Fred Weddington, manager of Security First National Bank along with his staff in Fiesta garb in front of the bank, 1940s. Courtesy The Weddington Family Collection

BELOW LEFT: Adohr Milk delivery truck, circa 1940. Courtesy CSUN

BELOW RIGHT: Van Nuys News employees and newsboys gather outside the newspaper building for a company photo in the 1940s. Courtesy Daily News Archives

RIGHT TOP: El Portal Theatre on Lankershim in North Hollywood in 1941. *Courtesy The Weddington Family Collection*

RIGHT BOTTOM: Sepulveda Boulevard looking north from Devonshire Street in 1942. Pacific Electric Tracks run down the middle of Sepulveda while a motorist gets a ticket at left. This section of track remained in place until the 1950s to service citrus packing plants on Brand Boulevard. Pacific Electric ran down the middle of Sepulveda from Parthenia to Brand Boulevard. *Courtesy Robert Peppermuller on behalf of the Craig Rasmussen Collection*

May 26, 1941

IMPETUS GIVEN GREAT FREEWAY FROM VALLEY TO CITY'S HARBOR

Forty miles of high-speed, non-stop travel connecting San Fernando Valley to Los Angeles Harbor Area, directly through metropolitan Los Angeles, is the latest freeway in Los Angeles County proposed to alleviate traffic congestion that has become one of the major problems of the county ... The high-speed artery is projected to be constructed along the Los Angeles River right-of-way from the harbor area to the San Fernando Valley connecting up with the Ridge Route to San Joaquin Valley.

Sept. 4, 1941

IT'S 35 MILES - OR ELSE

Effective right now, 35 miles an hour is the absolute top speed in Los Angeles city limits, unless the motorist wants to collect a ticket, warns Deputy Chief Bernard Caldwell.

ABOVE: National Defense Headquarters for the San Fernando Valley during WWII. Courtesy The Weddington Family Collection

LEFT: Bob Hope laughs with sidekick Jerry Colonna, left, at Burbank Airport in the 1940s. Courtesy The Weddington Family Collection

Dec. 9, 1941

UNITED STATES AT WAR WITH JAPAN

At 9:30 a.m. Monday, Dec. 8, 1941, Franklin D. Roosevelt, President of the United States, asked the Congress for a declaration of war on Japan. At 10:15 a.m. Monday, Dec. 8, 1941, Congress declared a state of war existed between the United States and Japan. Vote in the Senate was unanimous - 82 to 0. Vote in the Congress was 388 to 1 - the single adverse voted being that of Representative Jeanette Rankin of Montana. She was among the few that voted against war with Germany in 1917. Declaration of war against Japan was America's answer to the bombing in Hawaii by Japan, resulting in death and injury to hundreds of American soldiers. The attack occurred at 10:05 a.m. Sunday - 2 hours and 55 minutes before Japan declared war on the United States - at 1 p.m.

Jan. 13, 1942

VAN NUYS DISTRICT GETS 139 TIRES, 114 TUBES

The County Defense Council has released the tire and tube quotas for the month of January, declaring they would be rigidly enforced in the United States rubber rationing program ... The Van Nuys district, which includes all territory in the Valley west of Fulton Ave., is allotted 65 automobile tires and 54 tubes; 74 truck tires and 60 tubes.

LEFT TOP: Rotary Club baseball team. Lucy Fonseca, last on right and Ramona Fonseca, 3rd from right.
Courtesy Della Ortega

LEFT BOTTOM: Arthur Langton saws driftwood to be used as fuel in the home fireplace as a way to reduce dependence on natural gas. Courtesy Arthur Langton

OPPOSITE TOP: Harry and Peggy McKim were just two of the many dedicated North Hollywood citizens who volunteered their time and effort to the war cause. The McKim children collected newspapers and magazines for the Civil Defense Committee in Action, whose motto was 'in thought, in word, in action, be American,' and give.
Courtesy The Weddington Family Collection

OPPOSITE BOTTOM LEFT: Overhead view of the North Hollywood men and women of the Navy during a fund-raising effort by the Chamber of Commerce during World War II.
Courtesy The Weddington Family Collection

OPPOSITE BOTTOM RIGHT: U.S.O. on Lankershim Boulevard developed social events to meet with the service men during World War II.
Courtesy The Weddington Family Collection

July 7, 1942

SUGAR 'BONUS' COMING SOON

Cheer up, housewives. Here is good news. A sugar "bonus" or two pounds for every ration card holder purchasable between July 10 and Aug. 22 was announced by the office of Price Administration because of the somewhat heavier shipments of sugar into this country than anticipated.

ABOVE: Aerial view of Granada Hills looking north, circa 1944. All the rows are orange trees. Running north to south in a straight line is Balboa Avenue.
Courtesy Charles P. Myers

LEFT: Arthur Langton fishing in the Los Angeles River. Courtesy Arthur Langton

OPPOSITE: Street car lines can be seen above the streets in Glendale surrounding Bank of America, circa 1943.
Courtesy Daily News Archives

March 5, 1943

SUPPLIES OF FRESH FRUIT AND VEGETABLES VANISH

Demands for fresh fruit and vegetables to substitute for rationed canned foods have increased 50 percent - this, just as tomatoes, peas, and snap beans, in addition to onions and potatoes have become harder to get than ever before in Southern California. Tomatoes from Mexico, onions from Minnesota, and potatoes from Florida, are samples of Southern California's imports of fresh food, which heretofore the state always had produced in surplus, in the past.

July 20, 1943

VALLEY SEWER SYSTEM IMPROVEMENT COST SET AT $907,000

Elimination of cesspools in a large part of San Fernando Valley is seen in the announcement just made that the City Council has tentatively approved 22 projects dealing with sewer extensions and improvements, the total estimated cost of which is $907,000 ...

Feb. 3, 1944

VAN NUYS LAUNCHES 'RENT A SPARE ROOM' CAMPAIGN

As San Fernando Valley's critical housing shortage neared a new crisis with facilities needed immediately for 300 families of Army personnel in the area, a "rent your spare room" campaign was launched in Van Nuys this week. Pleas for rentals were made Sunday night at La Reina theatre in Sherman Oaks and the Van Nuys Theatre ... Those who volunteered their spare rooms during the show intermission were hailed as veritable heroes of the occasion, the audience applauding loudly and flash bulbs flaring.

RIGHT: Air raid drill at Lockheed in the 1940s.
Courtesy CSUN, Del Stelk Collection

OPPOSITE TOP: Cavalcade of Canoga Park participants, circa 1945. Courtesy Calabasas Historical Society

OPPOSITE BOTTOM: Ed Schlossman leads the race at a track meet for Loyola High School at Canoga Park, 1946. Courtesy Ed Schlossman

BELOW LEFT: Bob Hope with studio beauties at the Warner Bros. Studio lot, May 23, 1946. Courtesy CSUN

BELOW RIGHT: San Fernando Morningside Grammar School Girl Scouts. Left to right back row; Sharon Brock (1st), JoAnn Dux (4th), Sylvia Altman (5th), Sharon Decker (6th), Mary Ann Parton (8th). Front row; Beverly Hines (1st), Carol Lewis (2nd), Sally Barrett (4th), Dixie Carnes (6th), Carol Haines (7th). Courtesy Sharon Jackman

April 12, 1945

PRESIDENT SUCCUMBS

The nation's wartime leader, Franklin Delano Roosevelt, passed on today, leaving the nation stunned in the midst of its jubilation over the progress of the Allied Armies. Death came suddenly to the President. His passing drove all other matters from the minds of the people. Presses were stopped and radio programs shut off to record the tragic event. President Roosevelt's death occurred at 2:55 p.m. The President was at Warm Springs, Ga., where he went ten days ago. Death was attributed to cerebral hemorrhage. Services will be held at Hyde Park Sanctuary.

April 26, 1945

FARM LABOR SHORTAGE

The San Fernando Valley faces a serious farm labor shortage in view of a decision of Federal authorities to reduce by half the number of Mexican nationals that ranchers were expecting to employ during the summer. Because of that shortage, it is possible that German prisoners may be put to work here on other than the orange picking work they are assigned to thus far, A.F. Gillette, Assistant Farm Advisor reported.

May 10, 1945

ON TO TOKYO

Van Nuys citizens observed V-E Day most fittingly - in prayer and doing their regular chores. One person was so bold as to ask why there was not the hilarious celebrating that marked the armistice in World War I. That's an easy one - we were still very definitely in a war. There will be abundant reason to celebrate when we have polished off the barbarians that murdered our citizens at Pearl Harbor.

Aug. 16, 1945

VICTORIOUS!

Americans were considered "soft" when the Nipa made their sneak attack. And the Nazis had the same opinion when they piled in with Japan and declared war against us. We'd be mopped up in no time. But see what happened. Yanks carried the torch through North Africa, through Sicily and through Italy and on through France into the land of the "superior" race - to conquer it. In a few short months America built up the greatest war machine in history.

V-Day, May 8, 1945

FROM REIMS, FRANCE, AT 2:41 THIS MORNING THE ASSOCIATED Press flashed the unofficial news that the surrender of all German fighting troops had actually taken place at a little red school house which is the headquarters of General Eisenhower.

The surrender which brought the war in Europe to a formal end after five years, eight months and six days of bloodshed and destruction was signed for Germany by Col. Gen. Gustav Jodl (Jodl is the new chief of staff of the German army)

It was signed for the supreme Allied command by Lt. Gen. Walter Bedell Smith.

It was also signed by Gen. Ivan Susloparov for Russia and by Gen. Francois Sevez for France.

ABOVE: Lockheed workers celebrate the end of World War II as they finish their shift. Courtesy CSUN, Del Stelk Collection

May 9, 1946

DOBERMAN PUP SHOW FOR VETS

Veterans hospitalized at the Veterans' Administration Birmingham General Hospital in Van Nuys will witness a puppy match limited to purebred Doberman pinscher puppies Sunday afternoon. Many of the hospitalized boys have seen action with the Doberman pinschers of the K-9 Corps in war zones and have a high regard for the working ability of these dogs.

LEFT: Southern Pacific's 'Daylight Limited' train 98 crossing Devonshire Street in Chatsworth on its way from San Francisco to Los Angeles. Courtesy CSUN

BELOW: Repair and conversions of aircraft at Van Nuys Airport after the end of World War II. Courtesy CSUN, Ralph Samuels Collection

ABOVE: A celebratory concert is held in 1958 at Campo de Cahuenga, where the treaty ending the Mexican-American War was signed in 1847.
Courtesy San Fernando Valley Historical Society

RIGHT: Canoga Park Sunkist Citrus Fruit packing plant, circa 1947. Courtesy Canoga-Owensmouth Historical Society

OPPOSITE: Allen McDermitt, Standard Oil station manager standing with his hand on an Atlas tire.
Courtesy Kathleen Richardson

May 12, 1947

CARMELITES TO DEDICATE ENCINO SCHOOL STRUCTURE

Dedication of a reinforced brick school building with auditorium, erected by the Catholic Church at 17720 Ventura Blvd., Encino, at a cost of $150,000 takes place next Sunday at 11 a.m.

Feb. 27, 1947

STEADY CRIME INCREASE KEEPS POLICE ON JUMP

How a postwar crime wave is taxing the strength of the Valley police division is vividly shown in the Los Angeles police department's annual comparison of crimes. Robberies, for instance, increased 194 percent. Grand theft from motor vehicles increased 158 percent, grand theft in general increased 58 percent, petty theft from motor vehicles increased 34 percent and petty theft in general increased 28 percent. Burglaries increased 31 percent. The total number of crimes in the Valley during the last year ran 20 percent over the number for 1945.

May 29, 1947

DRIVE-IN THEATRE WITH 800-CAR CAPACITY PLANNED ON ROSCOE BLVD.

A deluxe drive-in theatre involving an estimated cost of $200,000, will be erected on the property recently sold by Frank Spichtig to Pacific Drive-In Theatres Inc., an associate company of California Drive-In Theatres Inc. Proposed site comprises 15 acres of ground fronting on the south side of Roscoe Blvd., between Sepulveda and Van Nuys boulevards.

Sept. 16, 1948

TEACHERS BLINKING; 10 TWIN SETS IN ELEMENTARY SCHOOL

To add to the general confusion of opening day no less than 20 twins registered at Van Nuys Elementary School, causing teachers to virtually "see double" as they greeted their new classes.

Pierce School of Agriculture Opens; First Students Commencing Classes

SEPT. 18, 1947

NO OTHER LEADING AGRICULTURAL SCHOOL IN THE UNITED States has had such a propitious start as the Clarence W. Pierce School of Agriculture is enjoying, Vierling Kersey, Superintendent of schools, told 100 young men assembled to register as its first students Monday morning.

The superintendent said that the new Canoga Park institution represents Los Angeles City's highest per capita investment, on the basis of enrollment, of any school in the city.

He told the incoming students that they and succeeding student bodies should seek to develop a commendable school tradition, particularly one having a foundation of helpfulness.

Dr. Pierce, former president of the Los Angeles City Board of Education, for whom the school was named, spoke in praise of the aspirations that had led his hearers to seek enrollment in the school.

He declared there was no higher calling than that for which the assembled youths would be trained, and that need for their services was evidenced by employment awaiting the school's graduates ...

First year work is being carried on in Quonset buildings and other temporary structures pending erection of the first group of eight permanent buildings to arise on the 400-acre site between Winnetka Ave. and De Soto Ave., north of Oxnard St. and south of Topham St.

Nov. 15, 1948

DAIRY, POULTRY INDUSTRIES YIELD TO ADVANCE OF POPULATION PROJECTS

Increase of population with resultant development of housing projects on land heretofore used for farming is steadily but surely robbing the San Fernando Valley of its famed dairy and poultry industries, a report of the county livestock inspector showed today. Present trend of home building probably will result in transforming the Valley from a highly productive agricultural section to an urban area with little if any agricultural importance, in the opinion of the inspector.

Jan. 13, 1949

ICE SKITTISH DRIVERS TROD EASY ON GAS

Though caught by surprise by the Valley's first snowfall in 16 years, local motorists drove cautiously enough to avoid the predicted rash of bad accidents ... Despite slippery slush and ice-covered streets, only three injury accidents involving vehicles occurred.

RIGHT TOP: Lila Martsch and her daughter, Nancy, enjoy a rare snowfall in the backyard of their home at 1806 Winona Avenue, January 1949. Courtesy Nancy Martsch

RIGHT BOTTOM: Kry's Market after heavy snow, February 1948. Courtesy Gary Krystof

OPPOSITE: Pierce College, 1948.
Courtesy San Fernando Valley Historical Society

ABOVE: Canoga Park High School PTA officers, Mrs. Ralph Graham, president, left, and Mrs. M.C. MacPherson, membership chairman, extend thanks to students Corky Tattersfield and Bob Westminster for their part in a membership drive in 1949.
Courtesy San Fernando Valley Historical Society

RIGHT: San Fernando Police Department connects directly with the Los Angeles sheriff's office through a new teletype service in 1949. Giving it a test are Chief Walter Heebing and policewoman Mary Muir. Courtesy San Fernando Valley Historical Society

May 2, 1949

WIFE NOT LIABLE WHEN HUBBY DOES BACK SEAT DRIVING, SO JUDGES RULE

When a husband is acting as a "back seat driver" and giving her orders, a wife at the wheel of the family car is not legally liable for what she may do! So ruled the Appellate Division of the Superior Court in an appeal of Mrs. Cora E. Stately of Inglewood, from a $10 fine she received for refusing to yield the right of way to a pedestrian. The woman contended that because her husband had informed her she had plenty of clearance and to "take it," she was not responsible because she had acted under specific orders from her husband.

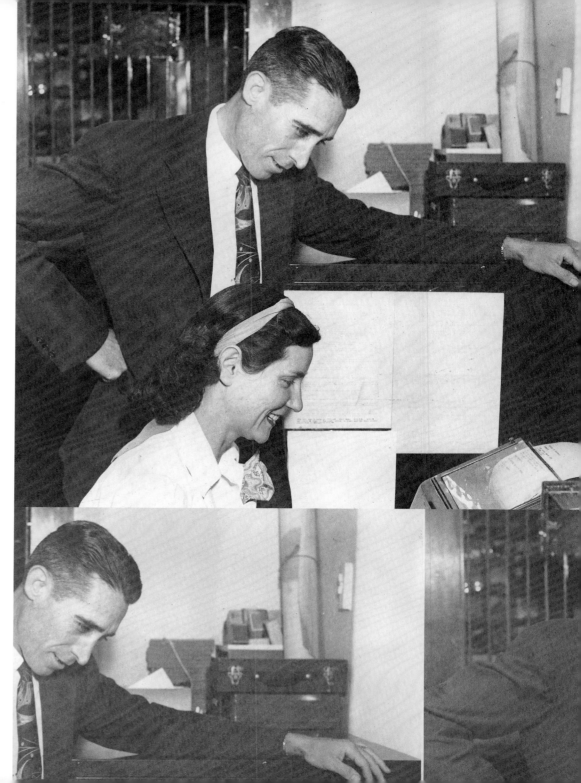

LEFT: Chicken Ranch sign with egg prices from 1949.
Courtesy Jack Textra

BELOW LEFT: A house near Van Nuys Airport is surrounded by a sea of mud after a heavy rainfall.
Courtesy Tom Piester

BELOW RIGHT: George Lupo with his wife Frances and children after the snow storm of 1949.
Courtesy Carla Adelmann

June 6, 1949

FIREMEN ANSWER 43 ALARMS IN DAY

Fanned by hot, dry winds, the tinder-dry Valley was the scene of more than 20 fires Friday, topped by a brush fire which engulfed almost a square mile of chaparral covered foothills south of Ventura Blvd. and west of Laurel Canyon Blvd. before it was brought under control by nearly 200 firefighters after a five-hour battle.

Sept. 5, 1949

CANOGA PARK BIDS FOR CHILD MENTAL HOSPITAL

Canoga Park businessmen and officials stand ready to aid the state locating a hospital for mentally deficient children within the boundaries or in the vicinity of that community, Gov. Earl Warren was told in a letter he received today from the Canoga Park Chamber of Commerce.

Oct. 13, 1949

WOODLAND HILLS FIREMEN READY

San Fernando Valley's newest fire station was opened this morning in Woodland Hills for fire-fighting service when "A" platoon of Station 84 went on duty at 5340 Canoga Ave. in the attractive $44,000 bungalow-type headquarters.

ABOVE: Supreme Council of the Mexican American Movement, Tujunga, May 1949. Courtesy CSUN, Supreme Council of the Mexican American Movement

The 1950s

THE 1950S SAW THE SAN FERNANDO VALLEY SOLIDIFY ITS role as the nation's quintessential suburb. Returning World War II veterans were now working men with families, a car and a mortgage. Middle-class neighborhoods seemed to spring up overnight – blocks of tidy bungalows and ranch houses squeezing out the orchards and farms that had given the region its early success.

Jobs were plentiful, and the possibilities were seemingly endless. Chevrolets rolled off the assembly line at the General Motors plant in Van Nuys. Anheuser-Busch invested $20 million in a brewery – the new "Budweiser home in the West." The Veterans Administration dedicated a hospital in San Fernando. The growth of television offered fresh opportunities in the entertainment industry. The Los Angeles Police Department opened new stations in North Hollywood, Reseda and Pacoima. Rocketdyne built rocket engines in Canoga Park and tested them — and an experimental nuclear reactor — at its top-secret hilltop lab above Chatsworth.

There were ample opportunities for younger residents, too. Two-year-old Valley College moved from temporary quarters on the Birmingham High campus to its permanent site in Valley Glen in 1951. That same year, Pierce College in Woodland Hills enrolled women for the first time. And in Fall 1956, San Fernando Valley State College opened on the former Halvorson Ranch in Northridge. Some 1,400 students attended classes in temporary bungalows while permanent facilities were built.

It was an innocent time, when the grand opening of the Sears & Roebuck at Valley Plaza in North Hollywood drew a crowd of thousands. Teenagers spent every Wednesday night cruising Van Nuys Boulevard. A close-knit Woodland Hills neighborhood started the holiday tradition of Candy Cane Lane, with elaborate themed displays in their front yards. A Granada Hills neighborhood was considered the perfect all-American community to show off to visiting Soviet Premier Nikita Krushchev (although he was angry at not seeing Disneyland and refused to get out of the car). Even the young actor who played the title role in the iconic '50s sitcom "Leave It to Beaver" hailed from the Valley.

The community also pulled together after a midair collision of a transport plane and a fighter jet 25,000 feet above Hansen Dam rained flaming wreckage onto the playground of Pacoima Middle School. Three young boys and five of the six crew members aboard the aircraft perished. Two years later, on Feb. 3, 1959, the Valley lost teenage rock 'n' roll singer Ritchie Valens of Pacoima, who died in an airplane crash that also claimed the lives of Buddy Holly and "The Big Bopper."

Another tragedy occurred in July 1959, although most people in the community were unaware of it. A partial meltdown at Rocketdyne's nuclear reactor released an undetermined amount of radiation. Company officials said at the time that no radiation had escaped and no one had been harmed. Three decades later, however, news of extensive radioactive and toxic contamination at the lab spurred a flurry of health-related lawsuits and calls for an extensive environmental cleanup that continue to this day.

— *Barbara Jones*

OPPOSITE: The Pacific Electric Red Car is on the move on Vineland Avenue in 1951. The electric-powered street cars are replaced by buses in December 1952.

Courtesy Raphael F. Long

ABOVE: Members of the Canoga Park High School PTA package homemade candy as gifts for the faculty in 1950. Pictured are, from left, Mrs. Ansel Breniman, Mrs. M.G. MacPherson, Mrs. John Skoog and Mrs. Fred Netherton.
Courtesy San Fernando Valley Historical Society

RIGHT: A view of the San Fernando Mall area after redevelopment, circa 1950.
Courtesy San Fernando Valley Historical Society

OPPOSITE: Aerial view of Hollywood.
Courtesy San Fernando Valley Historical Society

BELOW: The Sepulveda Veterans Administration Hospital, specializing in the treatment of peuropsychiatric patients, was dedicated on April 17, 1955.
Courtesy San Fernando Valley Historical Society

Feb. 13, 1950

VALLEY NOSE COUNT NEARS HALF MILLION

Population of the San Fernando Valley, including Burbank, is estimated at 456,000 in a survey covering 17 communities and prepared for the Van Nuys office of the California Dept. of Employment. Number of persons gainfully employed is estimated at 81,885 ... Aircraft manufacturing and the motion picture industry account for most of the employment figures in Burbank; aircraft and automobile manufacturing with allied repair services lead in the Van Nuys area. The aircraft manufacturing industry, followed by motion picture and aircraft and miscellaneous repair services account for 77.8 percent of the Valley's total industrial employment.

May 1, 1951

**CENSUS BREAKDOWN SHOWS
335,174 VALLEY POPULATION**

San Fernando Valley, including the Sunland-Tujunga area but excluding Burbank, has a population of 335,174, which includes 12,858 in the city of San Fernando. That is the preliminary report on the 1950 federal census, made available by breakdown today, and it shows a gain of 126,756 over the preliminary census report of 1940.

Sept. 3, 1951

VALLEY FAIR ATTENDANCE NEAR 60,000

Perfect country fair weather, good management and community cooperation "had combined today to bring the San Fernando Valley Fair at Devonshire Downs to a glorious record-breaking close ... High in the list of popular attractions were booths set up by 12 Valley communities, some to represent agricultural resources; and others to represent industrial arts. Chatsworth was awarded first place in these exhibits with Pacoima placing second and Granada Hills third. Sun Valley was awarded first place in industrial division judging, with Van Nuys second and San Fernando in third place.

Birmingham Is Ghost Town; Move To Beach Completed

JUNE 5, 1950

BIRMINGHAM HOSPITAL STANDS AS A GHOST TOWN TODAY — echoing corridors without an echo, bare or disheveled wards, beds collapsed and other mute evidence that the Veterans Administration has carried out the President's directive to a fare-thee-well, with the whole kit and ka-boodle moved to Long Beach.

The last patient was taken from Birmingham to the new Long Beach V.A. Hospital Friday. He was Eugene Roehlin, 42, a polio patient confined to an iron-lung for the past 22 months ... Roehlin followed 11 critically ill patients who had been removed to Long Beach on Thursday, together with the total patient population, and thus the mass evacuation of Birmingham was complete.

Only movers and required hospital personnel have been admitted to the 146-acre grounds since Thursday, and transfer of all equipment was expected to be completed over this weekend, with the "Closed" sign due to go up on the entrance this week ...

The Presidents's directive had been carried out, weeks of controversy and combined citizens' and veterans hard toll to the contrary notwithstanding.

As one boy pensively murmured as he watched Thursday's mass move start swinging through the gates: "And to think that all this would happen by one stroke of the pen."

ABOVE: The Veterans Administration opened Van Nuys General Hospital in 1944, and soon renamed it in honor of Brig. Gen. Henry Birmingham. Thousands of soldiers were treated there — many of them wounded in WWII. The VA closed the hospital in 1950, and the building was converted to Birmingham High School, which opened in 1953. Courtesy Daily News Archives

RIGHT: Brothers Joel and Steven Tator in 1950 at their home on Magle Avenue in Sherman Oaks. Courtesy Dan Tator

OPPOSITE LEFT: Ladies enjoying the sun at the Pickwick Recreation Center in Burbank. Courtesy JoAnn Schueller Cooke

OPPOSITE RIGHT: Valley communities displayed their civic pride with signs like this, welcoming visitors to Sherman Oaks, circa 1950. Courtesy San Fernando Valley Historical Society

RIGHT: Mrs. Jane Bartels, left, shows her slim and trim class of homemakers how to be graceful catching a basketball, 1950. From left are Mrs. Bartels, Esther Berdrow, Arva Wylie, Marion Serling, Nona Kingsbury, Catherine Conwell, Viola Medearis, Evelyn Phillips and Jean Osburn.
Courtesy San Fernando Valley Historical Society

BELOW LEFT: Lt. Governor Goodwin J. Knight, Rex Allen, and Johnny Grant at the opening of the California Theatre in Burbank, on December 13, 1950.
Photo by CSUN

BELOW RIGHT: Hidden Hills is just being developed when this photograph is taken in the 1950s. The gated community incorporated as a city in 1961.
Courtesy Calabasas Historical Society

ABOVE: The polo team in Calabasas enjoys some champagne in their trophies after a polo match in the 1950s. Courtesy Calabasas Historical Society

LEFT TOP: Mrs. Edward Olstyn, center, poses with North Hollywood High School students for a photo promoting the Hawaiian Breakfast at the Hollywood Bowl in August 1950. The students are, from left, Salley Silverberg, Joan Gairdner, Carol Yates and Marilyn Taylor. Courtesy San Fernando Valley Historical Society

LEFT BOTTOM: Five excited kids meet cowboy star Roy Rogers, a Valley resident, during a promotional appearance. Courtesy Diane Piester

May 22, 1952

OIL FLOW IN COMMERCIAL QUANTITY REPORTED ON WEST VALLEY RANCH

Oil in commercial quantity has been struck in two shallow wells on the 170-acre Knapp ranch at the west terminus of Vanowen St. in Canoga Park. The wells, less than the 1200 feet deep, are each producing more than 50 barrels a day ... Secrecy has surrounded operations which are the result of promotional work by W.J. "Bill" McCarthy, brother of Glenn McCarthy, widely known hotel man of Texas.

Oct. 9, 1952

STRONG ANTI-COMMUNIST RULES SET UP IN CITY SCHOOL SYSTEM

Thirty thousand Los Angeles City Board of Education employees, from part-time and temporary workers to top superintendents, today are in receipt of pamphlets outlining the new rules and regulations of the Board of Education relative to membership in the Communist Party and the obligation to answer questions concerning duties and loyalty.

LEFT TOP: West Valley Hunt Club at Hidden Hills in the 1950s. Courtesy Calabasas Historical Society

LEFT BOTTOM: Looking east on Sherman Way from Reseda Boulevard in the early 1950s.
Courtesy Calabasas Historical Society

OPPOSITE: Metropolitan Airport is renamed San Fernando Valley Airport in 1950. Now known as Van Nuys Airport, it is the nation's second-busiest general-aviation facility. Courtesy Daily News Archives

RIGHT TOP: City Councilman Robert M. Wilkinson and Chamber of Commerce members check plans to widen Reseda Boulevard in the 1950s.
Courtesy CSUN, Papers of the Reseda Chamber of Commerce

RIGHT BOTTOM: The North Hollywood Chamber of Commerce sponsored the award-winning 'Betsy Ross' float in the Tournament of Roses Parade.
Courtesy The Weddington Family Collection

BELOW: Congressman Richard Nixon brings his U.S. Senate campaign to Reseda and Van Nuys in 1950.
Courtesy CSUN, Papers of the Reseda Chamber of Commerce

Nov. 6, 1952

VOTERS TAB EISENHOWER, NIXON, HOLT AND HIESTAND

Valley voters followed the national trend in Tuesday's general election when they gave a majority of over 50,000 votes to Gen. Dwight D. Eisenhower and Sen. Richard Nixon, and comfortable margins to Joseph F. Holt in the 22nd Congressional Dist. and Edgar W. Hiestand in the 21st Dist.

Dec. 10, 1953

WOODLAND HILLS LIGHTING LAUDED

Have you seen Candy Cane Lane in Woodland Hills? Every home on Lubao Ave. (three blocks west of Corbin Ave., Lubao Ave. from Ventura Blvd. to Topham Ave.) is illuminated and each home has a theme. These include Christmas Wishes, The Night Before Christmas, Toyland Parade and others. It really is exceptional, Mrs. Helen Couzens, telephone Diamond 8-5695, is the woman who started Candy Cane Lane.

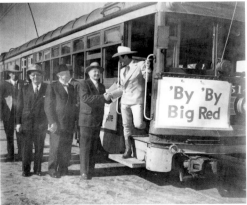

ABOVE: Manuel Bustamante and his son, Manuel Jr., fix up the front yard of their recently purchased home. The Budweiser plant is being built in the background. *Courtesy Annie Bustamante*

RIGHT: Jack Bailey and unidentified actresses on 'Queen for a Day,' a daytime game show that airs on television from 1956-64. *Courtesy The Weddington Family Collection*

June 24, 1954

OPEN NEW ANHEUSER-BUSCH $20,000,000 BREWERY

Official opening of Anheuser-Busch's new $20,000,000 Los Angeles brewery was held yesterday when state council and city officials participated with August A. Busch, president, and Eberhard Anhueuser, chairman of the board, in the official opening program ... Located just west of Sepulveda Blvd., on Roscoe Blvd., the new "Budweiser Home in the West" covers 65 acres. Construction operations started in December 1952.

ABOVE: Van Nuys residents visit the last of the large turkey farms in the Valley. The youngster bids the turkeys farewell shortly after Thanksgiving in 1953.
Courtesy CSUN, Ralph Samuels Collection

LEFT: A 'cats's whiskers' car tailors a railroad tunnel to handle oversize loads on April 23, 1954.
Courtesy San Fernando Valley Historical Society

BELOW: Joe and Thirza Bencivenga, and their children, Joyce and Joey, are photographed in 1956 at their home at 6504 Rhodes Avenue, North Hollywood. Courtesy Joyce Manahan

Aug. 12, 1954

$2 HAIRCUTS IN OFFING FOR MEN - OUCH!

Valley men were ruefully contemplating the prospect of $2 haircuts today after hearing from the general president of the Associated Master Barbers of America that the $1.50 price may soon be gone with the wind.

Jan. 20, 1955

CHOOSING 'MRS. VALLEY' AT BUTLER'S COOKING SCHOOL

Who will be the next Mrs. America? It may well be one of San Fernando Valley's outstanding homemakers, according to plans revealed today. Announcement is made that a community-wide contest will be conducted under the auspices of some of the Valley's leading civic organizations to select Mrs. San Fernando Valley ... Local homemakers, married, and 21 years or over are eligible to enter the 17th annual competition for the national title and more than $25,000 in prizes, it was disclosed.

RIGHT TOP: Painting of General Andres Pico by Orpha Hinker is unveiled in 1954. From left are Eldred L. Meyer, Orpha Klinker, Justice W. Turney Fox, Lt. Gov. Enrique Villegas Leyva, Mrs. Josephine Kemp and Mrs. Lillie Buchner.
Courtesy San Fernando Valley Historical Society

RIGHT BOTTOM: Owner Tom May breaks ground for the 452,000-square-foot May Company store at the Laurel Plaza mall in North Hollywood, 1954.
Courtesy The Wedding Family Collection

ABOVE: The North Hollywood Huskies dub themselves the "Uncrowned City Champions" in 1954. The team loses a coin toss to Wilson High for a shot at the city title. Manual Arts High defeats Wilson and wins the championship. The Huskies had beaten both teams during regular season play. Back row, from left Coach John Sanders, Dave Tanner, Tom Maudlin, John Lofstet, Bill Yapel and Coach John Trump. Front row, George Brooks, Ross Goodman, Guy McCreary, Al Howeser, Angie Nicademo, Joe Miller and Don Voyne. Courtesy The Wedding Family Collection

ABOVE: Actress Mara Corday unveils a picture of John C. Fremont at Campo de Cahuenga where California marked the anniversary of its admission to the union, 1955.
Courtesy San Fernando Valley Historical Society

RIGHT: An aerial view of the Golden State Freeway looking north shows the Hyperion Bridge in the foreground and Los Feliz Boulevard mid-picture. Riverside Drive is on the left, where the circular object at the intersection with Los Feliz is a fountain dedicated to William Mulholland.
Courtesy CSUN, Del Stelk Collection

Oct. 11, 1956

'NEWS' OPENS SECOND WEST VALLEY OFFICE

Keeping pace with the growth and development of its Central and West Valley circulation territory, The News and Green Sheet announces opening next Monday of its newest office at 7210 Jordan Ave., Canoga Park, to insure even more convenient personal service to West Valley readers and advertisers. Established in a more modern new store building, centrally located in the retail business district and across the street from Canoga Park Post Office, this office of The News will be completely staffed by representatives of the business, editorial, display and classified advertising departments.

ABOVE: Panoramic view of the rapid development of residential housing in the Sunland-Tujunga area of the San Fernando Valley in the mid-1950s. Courtesy CSUN

LEFT: Crooner Bing Crosby and unidentified actresses, 1956.
Courtesy San Fernando Valley Historical Society

May 18, 1957

CITY SCHOOL TEACHERS FAVOR SPANKING - WHERE IT'S NEEDED

A poll of 3750 teachers by the elementary needs committee of the Elementary Teachers Club disclosed nearly three-quarters of the instructors feel they should be allowed to administer "reasonable corporal punishment." The report to the Board of Education disclosed teachers feel pupils are misbehaving more than they did 10 years ago ... They said poor home training is the number one cause of disciplinary problems. Divorced parents, working mothers, over crowded classes, excessive teaching load and inadequate health services were listed as other causes.

Aug. 13, 1957

'SALARY IS FINE - BUT NOT OVERTIME,' SAYS IRATE WIFE

Mrs. Virginia M. Scales' belief her husband shouldn't have to work overtime landed her in Hollywood Jail, booked on suspicion of assault with a deadly weapon. When her husband John had to work Sunday in Frank O'Brien's electronic shop at 6514 Santa Monica Blvd., the 34-year-old Mrs. Scales of 1142 No. Poinsettia Place walked into the shop, picked up a handy two-by-four and clobbered O'Brien on the head, according to police.

TOP: USC Valley Trojans Club preparing for opening football game in 1957. Seen here are Miss James W. Gerig, Mrs. Robert K. Jones, Mrs. William R. Megowan and Mrs. E. William Sparr. Courtesy San Fernando Valley Historical Society

RIGHT: Mrs. William Allen, center, secretary of the Campo del Cahuenga Memorial Association, is flanked by Daughters of the American Revolution members Mrs. Helen Adams Neely, left, and Mrs. John Gilchrist, January 8, 1958. Courtesy San Fernando Valley Historical Society

FAR RIGHT: A view of property owned by Ed and Mildred Lombardi shows the Ventura Freeway being built in the background and a neighbor's private horseracing track in the foreground. Courtesy Rita Lombardi

March 27, 1958

TEACHER GROUPS CALL FOR PAY RAISES TO MEET LIVING COSTS

Request by Los Angeles teachers for a salary increase was being studied today by Supt. of Schools Ellis A. Jarvis. Two teacher groups, the American Federation of Teachers and the Affiliated Teacher Organizations of Los Angeles presented the requests to the Board of Education. Representatives of both organizations cited higher living costs as one of the major reasons for the need for increased pay. Raymond Blinn, representing the AFT, asked for a $5000 minimum and a $9130 maximum ... He said the median gross pay for a teacher is $6114 annually; yet the annual take-home pay is $4582 a year.

Aug. 3, 1958

VALLEY'S MOONWATCH STATION DESCRIBED BY EXPERT AS 'ONE OF FINEST' IN NATION

The Valley's Moonwatch station in Chatsworth, which tracks Russian and United States earth satellites is one of the finest in the country, according to a man who has visited more than a dozen states inspecting such installations. That man is Walter A. Munn, traveling field representative for the Smithsonian Institute Astrophysical Conservatory in Cambridge, Mass.

Aug. 10, 1958

MONROE HIGH SCHOOL OPENS SEPT. 15

Doors of the new James Monroe High School, 9229 Haskell Ave., Sepulveda, will open Sept. 15 to welcome 1800 assigned students, according to Dr. William J. Settle, principal. Although some of the buildings are not yet completed and the landscaping has not been done, sufficient classrooms will be finished to accommodate the expected enrollment, Dr. Settle said.

ABOVE: Workers from Morley Construction Company put the finishing touches on a billboard for San Fernando Valley State College, 1958. From left are Assemblyman Alan Miller; Dr. Howard S. McDonald, president of Los Angeles State College; and Dr. Ralph Prator, campus president. The college opened in 1956 with 1,400 students. Courtesy San Fernando Valley Historical Society

LEFT: The 1958 Pierce College Basketball Team. Included in photograph are Harley Rust, forward; Phil Faist, guard; Bruce Kielder, coach; Al Andreas, forward; Tom Ibersen, center; Roger Mix, guard. Courtesy CSUN

Dec. 11, 1958

NINE KILLED IN CULT HOME BLAST

An explosion which blew the Chatsworth canyon home of religious cult leader Krishna Venta to bits claimed the life of Venta and eight other persons early yesterday. One of the dead is believed to be an expelled member of the cult who brought a bomb into the area in a duffle bag. The nine bodies were burned beyond recognition and positive identification will have to be made from teeth, jewelry and in some cases fingerprints, according to Lt. R. M. Hollis of the Ventura County sheriff's office in charge of the investigation.

ABOVE: The Sherman Way underpass is completed in 1959 to accommodate an 8,000-foot-long runway at Van Nuys Airport. Courtesy Daily News Archives

Oct. 9, 1959

DODGERS CRUSH WHITE SOX TO BECOME WORLD CHAMPS

The Los Angeles Dodgers yesterday did what no other team in the history of baseball has done. After finishing seventh last year, the Dodgers won the world championship with a 9-3 victory over the White Sox in Chicago. The four games to two triumph for the Dodgers marked the first time a seventh place finisher the previous year had come back to a win the World Series.

ABOVE: Mae West sold her Van Nuys property to the John R. Thompson Company of Chicago. They are at the ground breaking with representatives, office managers and cafeteria personnel for the first Ontra cafeteria. Courtesy John Stotler

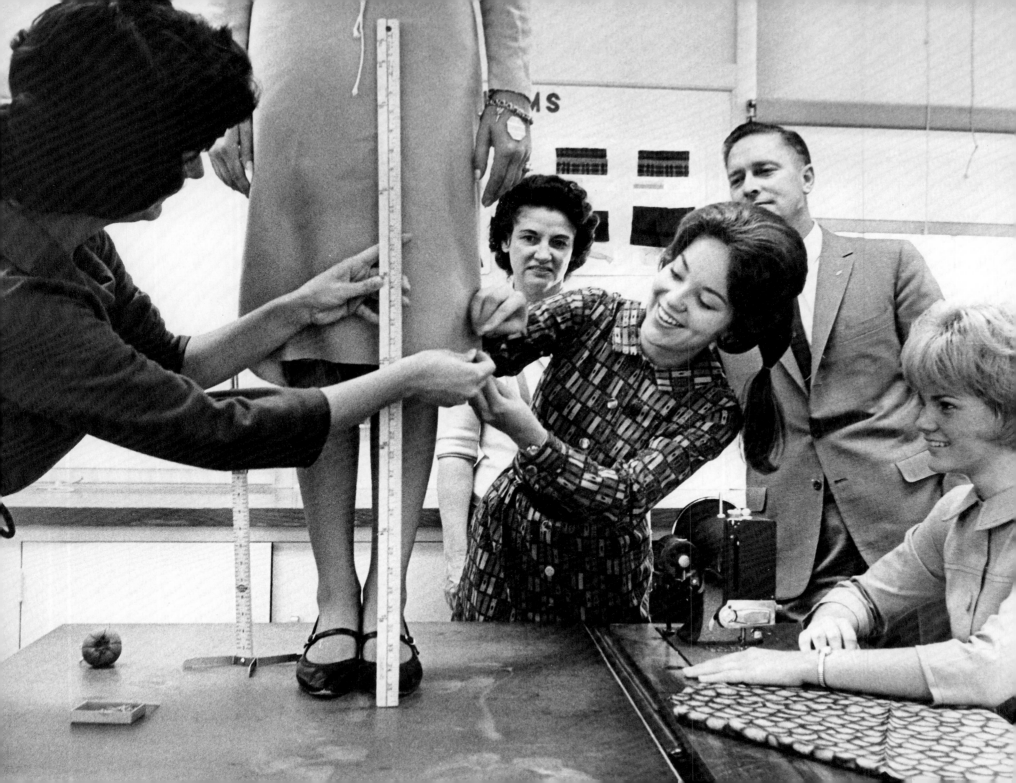

The 1960s

THE MAINSTREAM LIFESTYLE OF THE "FABULOUS '50" morphed into a counterculture in the 1960s, a decade marked by rebellion, violence, social protest and radical change. The generation gap was evident in the San Fernando Valley, where civic leaders pushed forward with their plans for suburban progress, while their children mobilized with a different vision of the political and social landscapes. The conflicts in the Valley were like those taking place in every community in America, although the region found itself playing a role in many of the decade's historic events.

Civil rights became a high-profile issue in the Valley, although the population was overwhelmingly white. Two years before his march on Washington, D.C., Dr. Martin Luther King Jr. spoke at Canoga Park High and preached two sermons at Woodland Hills Community Church. "Love your neighbor as you love yourself," King told the congregation in January 1961. In March 1965, a multiracial group of more than 400 peacefully marched for civil rights from Pacoima to Van Nuys. Five months later, Mayor Sam Yorty of Studio City had to cope with the racially motivated Watts Riots that left 34 people dead. In 1968, 150 students led by the Black Student Union took over the administration building at Valley State College. That sit-in and other protests led to an agreement to recruit more black and Latino professors and students.

There were other demonstrations against the draft and the Vietnam War. During a March 1968 campaign speech at Valley State College, presidential hopeful Bobby Kennedy drew boos from the crowd when he called for an end to student deferments and expressed support for the draft. Kennedy was gunned down three months later in the kitchen of the Ambassador Hotel, an attack that wounded an Encino teen standing nearby. "It was like a bloody massacre – unbelievable," Ira Goldstein told The Valley News and Green Sheet.

Two months before the phenomenon of Woodstock, more than 120,000 fans converged at Devonshire Downs fairgrounds for Newport '69, America's largest rock concert to date. Crowds who came to hear such psychedelic icons as Jimi Hendrix, Steppenwolf and The Byrds spilled over into Northridge and Granada Hills, trashing the communities and sparking demands from angry residents that such a situation never occur again.

One of the Valley's most shameful chapters came in August 1969, when Charles Manson and his "family" went on a murderous rampage that shocked the world. The ex-con and his followers had been squatting in a run-down house in Canoga Park and at the remote Spahn Ranch movie set above Chatsworth. Local residents said they'd felt terrorized by his scary demeanor.

Despite the upheaval of the 1960s, the Valley continued to prosper. The Ventura Freeway was dedicated at the start of the decade, easing the commute for the hundreds of thousands of commuters who called the Valley home. Busch Gardens opened a 17-acre theme park with a Polynesian theme. Topanga Plaza opened in July 1964 — California's first enclosed shopping mall – drawing residents to its modern department stores and indoor skating rink. The Valley Music Theatre debuted on Ventura Boulevard, a domed landmark offering the newly popular "in-the-round" seating. And when the Apollo missions took man to the moon, the spacecraft were powered by rocket engines designed and built by Rocketdyne.

— *Barbara Jones*

OPPOSITE: Mrs. and Mrs. Lou Richey watch a home economics demonstration during Parents Night at Birmingham High School, 1962. Michele Chole hems a dress while Debbie Brodrick works the sewing machine. Courtesy San Fernando Valley Historical Society

March 4, 1960

**VALLEY NARCOTIC PROBLEM IS
HIGHLIGHTED BY ARRESTS**

"I wanted to be known as a real cool guy. I didn't want them to think I was chicken."
So explained a 16-year-old Sepulveda boy who was arrested, along with 28 other
teenagers and 17 young adults in a two-month narcotics roundup in the San Fernando
Valley. It is an explanation often heard by Sgts. D.J. Carr and P.A. Brautovich of the
juvenile narcotics bureau. But it doesn't alter the facts. Another teenager has been
transformed into a juvenile delinquent through marijuana cigarettes.

RIGHT: Miss Flashbulb Queen, Cindy Swanson, is crowned by Miss Stop the Presses,
Rachael O'Blenis, with Professor of Journalism Erling Erlandson in the background, 1960.
Courtesy San Fernando Valley Historical Society

BELOW: A crowd gathers to watch the Monroe High School football team play, circa 1960.
Courtesy San Fernando Valley Historical Society

May 10, 1960

WAY OF LIFE IN VALLEY FACED WITH EXTINCTION

A way of life in the San Fernando Valley is on the verge of extinction. Acre upon acre of oranges, walnuts, alfalfa and horse ranches, which once cause the Valley to be fabled in song and verse, have been covered bit by bit with a sea of subdivision development commonly known as "urban sprawl." In 15 short years, the Valley's population growth has pushed the former days of "country living" back to the very fringes of the area, until only three large blocks remain - and even two of these face almost immediate transformation.

ABOVE: Vice presidential candidate Lyndon B. Johnson waves to the crowd during a campaign stop in the Valley in 1960. He is accompanied by Dr. Ralph Prator, left, president of Valley State College, and Sen. Clair Engle of California.
Courtesy San Fernando Valley Historical Society

LEFT: Holy Cross Hospital under construction, circa 1960. Courtesy San Fernando Valley Historical Society

BELOW: The Lombardi Family owns and operates the Woodland Hills amusement park known as Kiddieland from 1958 to 1963. This photo was taken from atop the Ferris wheel. Courtesy Susan Lombardi Zahoryin

ABOVE: A rocket engine for the space program is tested at the Rocketdyne Santa Susana Field Laboratory above Chatsworth, circa 1960. Nuclear reactors were also developed and tested at the top-secret hilltop site. Courtesy CSUN

RIGHT TOP: Beauty contestants for Miss Mission Hills, 1960. Courtesy San Fernando Valley Historical Society

RIGHT BOTTOM: Aerial view of the 101 Freeway being built through the Cahuenga Pass, circa 1960. The Laurel Canyon Boulevard bridge is in the center foreground. Courtesy Daily News Archives

OPPOSITE LEFT: Fire at Vons Market in 1960 at Van Nuys Boulevard near Vanowen Street. The site was the former home of W.P. Whitsett.
Courtesy CSUN, Ralph Samuels Collection

OPPOSITE RIGHT: Enriqueta Vacio, left, and Chelo Ramirez play their instruments at a 1961 celebration to commemorate the Treaty of Cahuenga signing on January 13, 1847. Courtesy San Fernando Valley Historical Society

Jan. 13, 1961

CIVIL RIGHTS NEGRO LEADER WILL LECTURE

The Rev. Martin Luther King Jr., well known leader in the Southern Negro's fight for civil rights, will speak on "The Future of Integration" Sunday at 8 p.m. in Canoga Park High School Auditorium, 6850 Topanga Canyon Blvd. Dr. King, who made headlines in the Montgomery, Ala. bus boycott and aroused national indignation last fall when he was arrested at a sit-in lunch counter demonstration in Atlanta, is being sponsored here by the Woodland Hills Community Church.

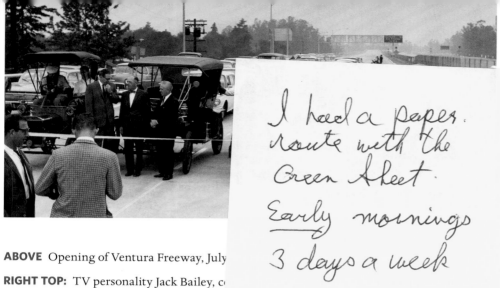

ABOVE Opening of Ventura Freeway, July...

RIGHT TOP: TV personality Jack Bailey, c... carrier in 1962. Courtesy Daily News Archives

RIGHT BOTTOM: Woodman Avenue Scho... make way for the Ventura Freeway. Students were a... Chandler School. Wayne Haserot is 4th from the left in the back row. Courtesy Barbara J. Menendez

OPPOSITE: Contestants of Mission Hills Beauty Pageant, 1963. Courtesy San Fernando Valley Historical Society

I had a paper route with the Green Sheet. Early mornings 3 days a week

Sept. 21, 1961

HIDDEN HILLS IS COUNTY'S NEWEST CITY

This picturesque residential community nestled at the foot of the Santa Susana Mountains across the Ventura Freeway from Calabasas, is Los Angeles County's newest and 73rd city ... It joins Rolling Hills to become the second city in the county with gate houses and private streets not open to public traffic. The move to incorporate was motivated by the fear the area would be annexed by the city of Los Angeles.

Aug. 7, 1962

PSYCHIATRIC TEAM PROBES DEATH OF MARILYN MONROE

A "suicide team" of psychiatrists and psychologists today is investigating to determine if the apparent overdose of sleeping pills that killed actress Marilyn Monroe was taken on purpose or accidentally. The 36-year-old blonde star was found dead in her Brentwood home early Sunday.

July 9, 1963

NEGROES DEMAND SCHOOL INTEGRATION BY SEPTEMBER

Racial integration by September! That in effect, was the ultimatum handed to the Los Angeles City Board of Education by the National Association for the Advancement of Colored People. The request was made by three spokesmen for the Negro organization at a special meeting of the board's ad hoc committee on racial integration, of which Mrs. Georgiana Hardy is chairman.

Nov. 26, 1963

FEW PEOPLE ON QUIET VALLEY STREETS; IT WAS A SAD DAY

Yesterday would have been a regular work day except for one thing, that President Kennedy was buried at Arlington Cemetery. Everyone spoken to by a roving "News" reporter said it was a sad day ... There wasn't a boat in Hansen Dam lake. Had it been any other time of day the waters there would have been churning with speed boats and water skiers, and several hundred would have been fishing around the banks of the lake.

TOP: Birmingham High School seniors get together for the last time as classmates at their graduation night party in 1963. Courtesy San Fernando Valley Historical Society

RIGHT Valley State's Ollie Carter, who was the leading scorer in the CCAA in 1964, shows off his defensive ability against Jim Olsen of Cal Lutheran College. Courtesy San Fernando Valley Historical Society

FAR RIGHT: Seymour Mann, president of the Industrial Association of the San Fernando Valley, reports on the region's new industries, 1962. Pictured, from left, Ralph Goodson, William Bailey, Walter Harman, Mann and Jack Rohring. Courtesy Valley Industry and Commerce Association

ABOVE: Taft High players known as 'The Flying Irishmen' play in 1965. They are Tim O'Brien (81), Tony Boyehento (61), Dave Crane (51), Chuck Mortenson (54) and Steve Landress (65). Courtesy Herb Carleton

LEFT TOP: Encino businessman Al Borkin donates $3,000 to the Birmingham Stadium Fund. Also pictured are actors Dick Van Dyke, left, and Dennis Weaver. Courtesy San Fernando Valley Historical Society

BOTTOM LEFT: Patricia Doherty and her attorney, Grant Cooper, after her acquittal in March 1965 in the fatal shooting of her husband, Robert. Doherty testified that she'd been terrorized throughout her marriage and acted in self-defense when she shot her husband eight times. Courtesy San Fernando Valley Historical Society

BOTTOM RIGHT: Aerial view of 5 Freeway and Colorado Boulevard. Large white roof building is now Quixote Studios, formerly Electronic Specialties, Telemetry Division. Courtesy Bill Reagan

March 14, 1965

HUNDREDS JOIN IN 12-MILE VALLEY CIVIL RIGHTS MARCH

More than 400 Negroes and whites participated in a 12-mile peaceful civil rights march in the Valley yesterday, which started in Pacoima and concluded at the steps of the Valley Municipal Building in Van Nuys where the demonstrators were addressed by their leader ... The marchers arrived in Van Nuys at 4:30p.m. singing "We Shall Overcome."

Oct. 15, 1965

'IT'S GETTING TO BE A HABIT' - DODGERS WIN ANOTHER SERIES

Sandy Koufax and his Dodgers have brought the professional baseball's world championship to Los Angeles for the third time since the club's big move from Brooklyn in 1958. Koufax, possibly the best pitcher in the history of the game, shut out Minnesota's usually hard hitting Twins in the seventh and deciding game of the World Series yesterday at Bloomington, 2-0, getting a big defensive assist from Jim Gilliam.

RIGHT TOP: General Motors workers celebrate the 2 millionth vehicle assembled at the Van Nuys factory, March 1965. The plant opened in 1947, and manufactured Chevrolets and Pontiacs until it closed in 1992. Courtesy CSUN, Ralph Samuels Collection

RIGHT BOTTOM: Van Nuys Rotary 1960-65. Local businessmen are seen here.
Courtesy CSUN, Ralph Samuels Collection

Busch Gardens Sets May 26 Opening Date

THE $4,000,000 BUSCH GARDENS IN VAN NUYS WILL BE thrown open to the public Thursday, May 26, at 1 p.m. at 15840 Roscoe Blvd., where a man-made transformation in less than three years has turned a sandy lot into a fantasy-land which, even in anticipation, is spoken of in much the same tone as Disneyland … All of those who care to come and see will be invited to see vistas of bluelake, green islands, quaint, half-hidden arched bridges; jungle of palm and fernery; tall trees, an eagle's lair, and a 45-foot waterfall.

Also, boats carrying 22 passengers that traverse the streams on an unseen underwater rail, amphitheater, pavilions, a 3500-foot monorail line and a remarkable collection of trained tropical birds.

The birds provide an entertainment tour de force on the Busch Gardens program. Melvin Clinton, the birdmaster has his charges counting, singing, charging, doing almost everything but playing pinochle.

The Gardens' opening, just three and one-half weeks away, will bring to actuality a dream which led up to the first bite of a golden plow, pulled by the famous Anheuser Busch hitch of eight Percheron horses, in August 1963 … Six-and-a-half acres of the Gardens will be water, stocked with fish. Islands go under the names of Palm and Flamingo, descriptive of their character.

One of the lagoons stretches, cooler than others, will be home to otters and penguins.

Boats which traverse the lagoons and circle the islands will, alone of all attractions, include a charge to the public. It will be nominal — 25 cents.

The 3500-foot monorail, which gives a birds-eye look at almost everything as it skirts about and above

the Gardens' attractions will also ply through the brewery itself and provide a similar look at the spic and span ways in which the brewery carries its malt and hops through safeguarded phases of brewing.

Polynesian plantings, thickets of bamboo, palms and flowering exotics will provide visitors with bowers of exciting view.

Jan. 18, 1966

VALLEY LEADS NATION IN REAL ESTATE SALES FOR 9TH STRAIGHT YEAR

Despite its phenomenal growth in all phases of urban development, the Valley still is considered the "world's largest bedroom" area. And supporting this status is the disclosure that the San Fernando Valley Board of Realtors Inc. for the ninth consecutive year continues to lead the nation's 1500 board of Realtors in total residential sales volumes.

LEFT: A visitor pets a parrot at Busch Gardens, an amusement park that operates adjacent to the Anheuser-Busch Brewery in Van Nuys from 1966-79. Photo by Jeff Goldwater/Los Angeles Daily News

BELOW: Roman Gabriel, a former quarterback for the Los Angeles Rams, autographs a photo for Bruce Adelstein, who is seated in his lap. Courtesy Brian Adelstein

Jan. 6, 1967

REAGAN TELLS PLANS IN INAUGURAL SPEECH

Ronald Reagan outlined his plans for a "Creative Society" yesterday morning in his inaugural address as California's 33rd Governor ... Gov. Reagan devoted much of his address to the problem of tax reform and how to achieve a balanced budget.

Jan. 29, 1967

CITY'S POPULATION CONTINUES TO SOAR; VALLEY LEADS WAY

Los Angeles' population has soared to nearly 3,000,000 - with the Valley leading in the population boom, ... The report showed an increase of 31,000 in the Valley, greatest growth area over the period of October 1965 to October 1966, in comparison with three other designated areas of the city.

May 2, 1967

CBS WILL MAKE MOVIES IN VALLEY

Announcement of Studio City's return as a center for motion picture production for the world's movie houses, and along with this, news that $20,000,000 to $25,000,000 a year will be infused into the Valley's economy - most of it right in Studio City - was heralded to members of the Studio City Chamber of Commerce ... The $9,500,000 outright purchase of the CBS Studio Center, climaxing CBS' leasing of the ex-Republic, ex-Mack Sennett studio complex at 4024 Radford Ave., was now wholly wrapped up after 60 days in escrow, and the completion of the purchase has opened the door to big, new, far-reaching plans.

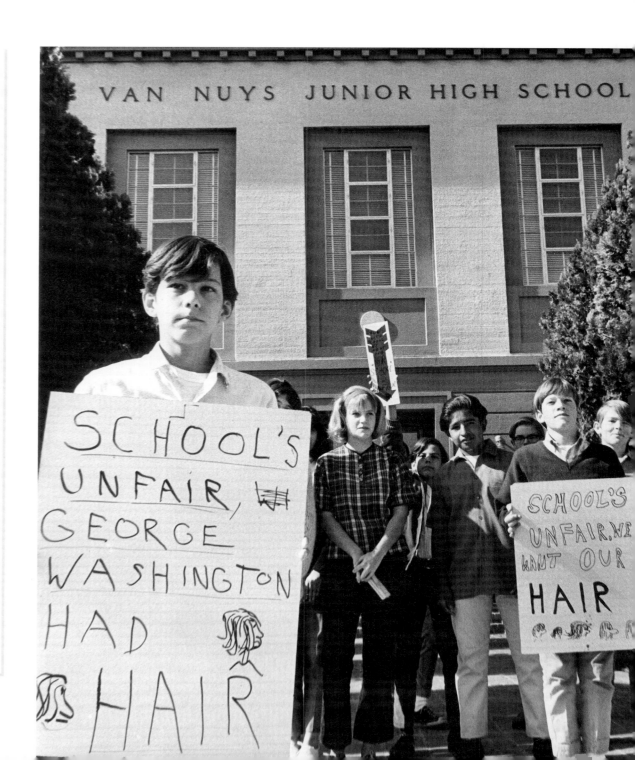

LEFT: Jubilant over plans for the dedication of multimillion-dollar Reseda Boulevard grade separation, four of the planners wave to members of the Northridge Chamber of Commerce, 1967. The four are standing at the rear of a private railcar owned by J.H. Long, superintendent of the Los Angeles Division of Southern Pacific Railway. From left are Nils Oberg, vice president of Oberg Construction Co.; City Councilman John P. Cassidy; Chamber President Neill Lehr; and Long.
Courtesy Daily News Archives

OPPOSITE: Students at Van Nuys Junior High demonstrate against a policy banning long hair on boys, circa 1967. Courtesy San Fernando Valley Historical Society

BELOW LEFT: Dan Richardson, disc jockey for Los Angeles Valley College radio station KLAV.
Courtesy Kathleen Richardson

BELOW RIGHT: Chamber of Commerce President Eddie Holohan and Miss North Hollywood pose with Dodger pitching ace Sandy Koufax during Dodger Day, 1967. Courtesy The Weddington Family Collection

ABOVE: The Medina Family restaurant on Ventura Boulevard in Woodland Hills, now the home of Brother's Sushi. Courtesy Jim Medina

RIGHT TOP: Presidential candidate Robert Kennedy gives a speech at San Fernando Valley State College on March 25, 1968. Lesss than three months later, he is fatally shot at the Ambassador Hotel. Courtesy CSUN

RIGHT BOTTOM: By 1968, the Ventura Freeway stretches the length of the San Fernando Valley. Courtesy The Weddington Family Collection

OPPOSITE: Pressroom of the Valley News in Van Nuys, circa 1968. Courtesy Daily News Archives

March 26, 1968

15,000 HEAR KENNEDY TALK AT VALLEY STATE IN BID FOR NOMINATION

There was a less than enthusiastic reaction when Sen. Robert F. Kennedy told a crowd of nearly 15,000 at Valley State College that he supports the draft and an end to student deferments, but hearty approval overshadowed the boos when he added that he intends "to tell it like it is." Despite statements on the draft which are unpopular among many students, shouting supporters asked for autographs, buttons from his clothing, cuff links and the carnation in his coat lapel - and got them.

June 9, 1968

SORROW FILLS FUNERAL HOURS OF RFK

Sen. Robert F. Kennedy was eulogized yesterday in Los Angeles as a man who "lived hard and died hard." Almost five days after the Senator was shot, the impact he had made on Los Angeles residents became more and more evident.

Nov. 5, 1968

VALLEY STATE DEMONSTRATORS HOLD BUILDING FOR 4 HOURS

More than 150 students led by members of the Black Student Union yesterday occupied the upper four floors of the Administration Building at San Fernando Valley State College for about four hours and threatened administrators and secretaries with violence.

June 27, 1969

NICKEL ICE CREAM CONES MELT AWAY

Ice cream lovers took a licking on Monday when a major Southern California drugstore chain announced that its historic 5-cent ice cream cone had melted away forever. Inflation, in scooping down upon the ice cream counter, ended a 16-year era of nickel cones, raising prices from 5 to 10 cents for a double scoop.

West Valley Museum

ABOVE: Miss Teen finalists, San Fernando Valley, 1969. Front row from left to right, Michelle Murray, 18, Miss Teen Calabasas; Judi Beauchamp, 16, Miss Teen Canoga Park; Helen Perry, 15, Miss Teen Sepulveda; Vicki Olson, 18, Miss Teen Van Nuys; Margaret Hall, 16, Miss Teen Chatsworth; back row, from left, Terry Scott, 15, Miss Teen Reseda; Patricia Dunivant, 16, Miss Teen Sherman Oaks; Colleen McNamara, 15, Miss Teen Burbank; Marianne Ludwig, 16, Miss Teen Northridge; Karen Pulsko, 18, Miss Teen Woodland Hills; DeDe Schmitz, 18, Miss Teen Granada Hills and Lynn Lightfoot, 16, Miss Teen West Van Nuys, are among the finalist in the Miss Teen Western United States competition to be held in the Hollywood Palladium at Teen-Age Fair Pop Expo '69. *Courtesy CSUN*

RIGHT: Aerial view of Universal City in 1969, including the Universal Hilton in the foreground. This was the Valley's first big hotel. *Courtesy Daily News Archives*

The 1970s

THE REBELLION OF THE '60S DEMONSTRATED THE POWER OF community – a lesson that carried over as residents of the San Fernando Valley faced the challenges of the 1970s. They learned to pull together in a crisis, to vote for what they wanted and to organize against what they opposed. The complex issues – soaring taxes, rising crime and school integration – brought changes to the nation's biggest suburb.

Valley residents faced their biggest challenge in 1971, when a 6.6-magnitude earthquake leveled much of Sylmar, including the month-old Olive View Hospital. Just four months later, a methane gas explosion in an underground water tunnel in Sylmar killed 17 workers, the worst tunnel disaster in the state's history. In both instances, the community rallied to support victims, restore neighborhoods and rebuild lives.

A temblor of a different sort rattled the political landscape when Mayor Sam Yorty of Studio City was unseated by Tom Bradley in 1973, giving Los Angeles its first African-American mayor. Bradley's inauguration included a parade that emphasized the city's multicultural population, an effort to diffuse the racial acrimony of the campaign. Another upset came with the taxpayer revolt of 1978, when angry and frustrated homeowners statewide overwhelmingly approved Proposition 13, which put a limit on property taxes.

However, no issue was as divisive as that of school busing. In 1978, some 15 years after a lawsuit was filed seeking to end racial segregation in Los Angeles' public schools, the school board approved a busing plan affecting dozens of Valley campuses. While an Encino-based group called Bustop challenged the plan in court, thousands of parents enrolled their youngsters in private schools or moved away from Los Angeles. Busing ended in the early 1980s after another court ruled that busing could be ordered only when segregation was deliberate.

Other changes took effect in the 1970s that weren't earth-shattering, but affected Valley culture nevertheless. The Chamber of Commerce called an end to the tradition of Wednesday night cruising on Van Nuys Boulevard. Valley State College officially became California State University, Northridge, a change that earned it the colloquial moniker CSUN. A group of 150 civic leaders declared war on the slew of pornography-oriented operations springing up in the Valley. And the chief of the LAPD's Valley Bureau expressed concern about the soaring murder rate and the "social disintegration" behind the trend.

Finally, in the late 1970s, a group of disaffected Valley residents mounted an effort to secede from Los Angeles. The movement was squelched by the Legislature, which passed a law barring city formation without the approval of the City Council.

— *Barbara Jones*

OPPOSITE: The powerful San Fernando Earthquake hits at 5:59 a.m. on February 9, 1971, killing 65 people, including two motorists who are crushed in the collapse of a Golden State Freeway overpass. The temblor causes some $500 million in damage. The disaster is also known as the Sylmar Earthquake because it destroys the new Olive View Hospital in Sylmar. Courtesy Daily News Archives

Quake - 30 Reported Killed; Damage In Millions

A KILLER QUAKE THAT STRUCK THE LOS ANGELES METROPOLI-
tan area at 5:59 a.m. today apparently hit the hardest in
the North Valley area where loss of life and property
damage is staggering.

Hospitals — especially the Olive View and San Fernando Veterans Administrations facilities — were scenes
of death and destruction.

Supervisor Warren M. Dorn visited the Olive View
Hospital and described the new $28,000,000 facility as a
"total wreck."

The death toll throughout Los Angeles had reached
30 by 5 p.m. today, and much of this total is in the San
Fernando Valley.

Adding to the grim toll is the announcement that
workers at VA Hospital fear that approximately 40 per-

sons believed trapped in rubble will not be rescued alive.

Eight hundred sixty-two people have been reported
injured.

A reporter for The News was at the VA Hospital and
said he counted seven dead, and rescue teams were still
probing the ruins.

Ten surgeons from Harbor General Hospital were
sent to aid persons trapped in the wreckage.

Hospital officials were giving morphine injections
to some patients trapped in the wreckage. The rescuers
could reach these injured patients but were unable to
move them.

There were reports that some patients were removed
early in the morning at both Pacoima Memorial Lutheran and Holy Cross Hospitals.

Throughout the Los Angeles area, and especially in

the North Valley the quake left a path of destruction.

Granada Hills was described as one of the hardest
hit areas.

The quake itself measured 6.5 on the Richter Scale.
A reading of 6 is regarded as a major temblor.

Experts of the Caltech Seismology Laboratory said
the quake centered about 10 miles east of Newhall.

ABOVE: The Sepulveda Veterans Administration
Hospital lies in ruins after the San Fernando
Earthquake. Photo by Wally Fong/AP

LEFT: Workers remove patients' belongings and
medical equipment from the rubble of Olive View
Hospital, which opened just a month before the 1971
earthquake. Courtesy Daily News Archives

ABOVE: A section of the Golden State Freeway in Sylmar after the earthquake. Courtesy Daily News Archives

LEFT: The Golden State Freeway at the Foothill overcrossing on the day of the quake. Courtesy Daily News Archives

FAR LEFT: A news helicopter flies over a quake-damaged section of the Van Norman Reservoir. Fears of flooding force the evacuation of some 40,000 residents. Courtesy Daily News Archives

RIGHT: Vice President Spiro Agnew visits quake-damaged areas of the San Fernando Valley. Courtesy Daily News Archives

BELOW LEFT: The earthquake touches off fires around the Valley, including this blaze on Wicks Street in Sun Valley. Courtesy Daily News Archives

BELOW RIGHT: Rescue workers use heavy equipment in their search for quake survivors. Courtesy Daily News Archives

Feb. 9, 1971

CALL DRINKING WATER SAFE IN SPITE OF DISCOLORATION

Earthquake damage has brought about discoloration of the domestic water supply in portions of the Valley but there is no cause for alarm, Robert V. Phillip, engineer in charge of water works for the Department of Water and Power, reported today.

March 30, 1971

DEATH RULED FOR MANSON, THREE GIRLS

Charles Manson and three female members of his strange nomadic cult were condemned to death yesterday for the 1969 mass murders of actress Sharon Tate and six other persons. The verdict by a jury of seven men and five women ended a raucous, marathon trial that spanned more than nine months. The jury had spent 10 hours of deliberation over two days before returning the verdict against Manson, 36, Susan Atkins, 22, Patricia Krenwinkel, 23, and Leslie Van Houten, 21.

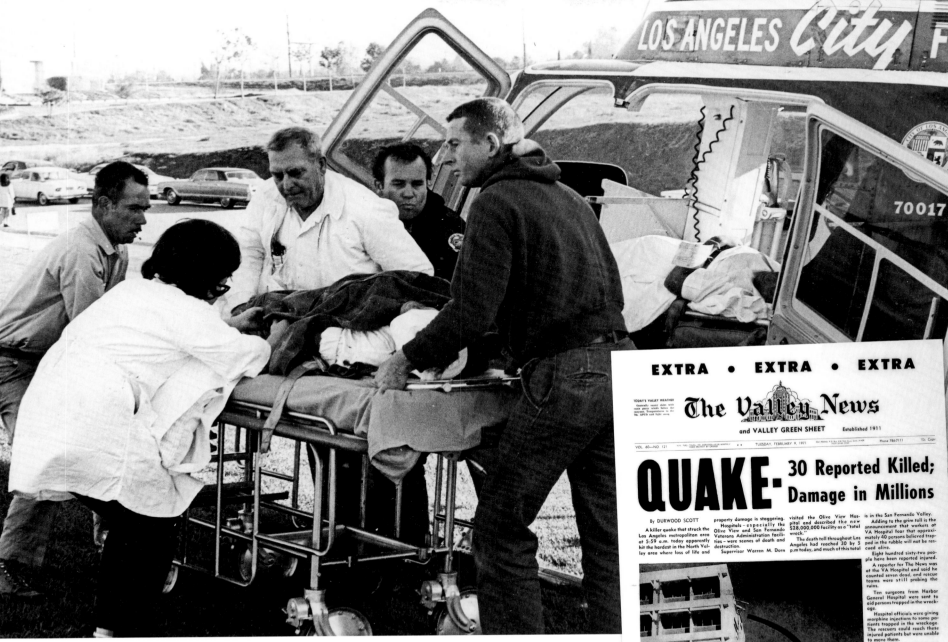

ABOVE: Rescue teams from Van Nuys Fire Department treat the injured in the wake of the Sylmar Earthquake of 1971. Courtesy CSUN, Ralph Samuels Collection

EXTRA • EXTRA • EXTRA

TODAY'S VALLEY WEATHER

The Valley News
and VALLEY GREEN SHEET   Established 1911

VOL. 60—NO. 121   TUESDAY, FEBRUARY 9, 1971   Phone 786-7111   10c Copy

QUAKE- 30 Reported Killed; Damage in Millions

By DURWOOD SCOTT

A killer quake that struck the Los Angeles metropolitan area at 5:59 a.m. today apparently hit the hardest in the North Valley area where loss of life and property damage is staggering.

Hospitals – especially the Olive View and San Fernando Veterans Administration facilities – were scenes of death and destruction.

visited the Olive View Hospital and described the new $28,000,000 facility as a "total wreck."

The death toll throughout Los Angeles had reached 30 by 5 p.m today, and much of this total

is in the San Fernando Valley.

Adding to the grim toll is the announcement that workers at VA Hospital fear that approximately 40 persons believed trapped in the rubble will not be rescued alive.

Eight hundred sixty-two people have been reported injured.

A reporter for The News was at the VA Hospital and said he counted seven dead, and rescue teams were still probing the ruins.

Ten surgeons from Harbor General Hospital were sent to aid persons trapped in the wreckage.

Hospital officials were giving morphine injections to some patients trapped in the wreckage. The rescuers could reach these injured patients but were unable to move them.

There were reports that some patients were removed early in the morning at both Pacoima Memorial Lutheran and Holy Cross Hospitals.

Throughout the Los Angeles area, and especially in the North Valley the quake left a path of destruction.

Granada Hills was described as one of the hardest hit areas.

The quake itself measured 6.5 on the Richter Scale. A read-

Call Drinking Water Safe In Spite of Discoloration

Jan. 28, 1972

BOARD OF EDUCATION REFUSES TO BAR CORPORAL PUNISHMENT

Dr. Robert Doctor's three-month campaign to get corporal punishment prohibited in the Los Angeles Unified School District was defeated by a 4-3 vote of the Board of Education yesterday.

Feb. 20, 1972

REACTIONS VARY AS CAL. SUPREME COURT ENDS DEATH PENALTY

The threat of execution has been lifted from the heads of some of the state's most notorious killers with the ruling by the California Supreme Court on Friday that the death penalty is unconstitutional. Barring a constitutional amendment, a rehearing by the State Supreme Court of a successful appeal to the U.S. Supreme Court, such infamous convicts as Charles Manson and Sirhan have escaped capital punishment ...

RIGHT TOP: A view of North Hollywood with Ventura Boulevard in the foreground, circa 1948. At right is what would become the community of Toluca Lake in 1973. Courtesy The Weddington Family Collection

RIGHT BOTTOM: Demolition of the old office building of the Glendale United School District in 1972. Courtesy Daily News Archives

LEFT TOP: Actress Irene Ryan, flanked by 'Beverly Hills' co-stars Max Baer Jr. and Buddy Ebsen, accepts a plaque from Cedars-Sinai Medical Center, 1974. Courtesy San Fernando Valley Historical Society

LEFT BOTTOM: Comedian Jerry Lewis gives the commencement address to the Class of 1974 at Notre Dame High School in Sherman Oaks. Courtesy Kathleen Richardson

Jan. 28, 1973

CEASE-FIRE SIGNING HALTS VIETNAM WAR; U.S. DRAFT STOPPED

More than 12 years of American fighting in Vietnam came to a halt yesterday at 4 p.m. PST with the signing of the cease-fire agreement in Paris. In Washington, Secretary of Defense Melvin R. Laird announced an immediate end to the draft five months before it was scheduled to expire on June 30 ... Some 522 troops, including one American, were reported killed in the 11th hour fighting. The Pentagon yesterday began the task of contacting the families of known American prisoners of war.

March 10, 1974

LUCILLE BALL RETIRES FROM TV SERIES

Lucille Ball has been the best. In the quarter-century of network television Lucy has been its queen. For 23 years, her show has been at or near the top. Her "I Love Lucy" series invented a new art form - the situation comedy. No single performer has ever dominated an entertainment medium with the verve and charm of the irrepressible redhead. And now it is over with Lucy's announcement to quit the weekly sitcom. But then no man or woman worked harder or longer than Lucille who, at age 62, continues to pour all her energies into every performance. She has been the most professional of them all. Never arrogant nor pretentious on or off the air. Lucy has been the ultimate television star.

Nov. 23, 1975

GROUP DECLARES WAR ON PORNOGRAPHY IN VALLEY

A gathering of nearly 150 persons from all over the Valley has declared war on prostitution and pornography oriented operations that have sprung up at an alarming rate in the Valley, according to police.

RIGHT: Dr. Carl Dentzel and Dale Evans, Western singer and actress, at the dedication of the Pioneer Church in Oakwood Community Park, 1976. Courtesy Daily News Archives

BELOW LEFT: Teens cuise Van Nuys Boulevard on a Wednesday night in 1977. The weekly cruise night was a tradition for more than 20 years. Courtesy Daily News Archives

BELOW RIGHT: The Valley News displays a new billboard erected throughout the Valley area to emphasize dramatic new changes in the Valley News in 1977. Witnessing the massive project, from left, are J. Scott Schmidt, president of the Valley News; Thomas Osborn, vice president, circulation; Richard Butler, president of Hall, Butler, Blatherwick Advertising, agency for the Valley News; Thomas Culligan, vice president, advertising of the News, and Dennis Hahn, account executive of Hall, Butler, Blatherwick Advertising. Courtesy Daily News Archives

The Valley's Daily Newspaper

Valley News

FINAL EDITION

VOL. 67—NO. 42

Saturday, September 10, 1977

© 1977 Van Nuys Publishing Co. 10c copy

Saturday —A day to remember!

Welcome to the first Saturday edition of the Valley News, another milestone in its 66-year history. You'll find many new elements in it, tailored specifically for your fast-moving lifestyle. But some things haven't changed. All of what you've come to expect are here, expanded, improved, easier to read. All together, we feel the Saturday package is unique. It will become part of your Saturday habit. Below are some of the special things you'll find in today's paper — and in the six days that follow.

Saturday Living, Real Estate, Leisure —See Section 2

Full stock tables in business section —Section 3, page 7

Preps and colleges in the Football tab —And the pros too

See weekend bargains first in classified —Section 3, page 16

Valley News photo by Herb Carleton

New season opens today

Like Charles White and his USC teammates, the Valley News will begin a brand new "season" today with its first-ever Saturday issue. New sports features, along with up to date football coverage, start today. White, the former San Fernando High School star, leads USC against Missouri today in season opener. See story in section 3, page 1.

What new morality?

L.A. politicos get share of junkets

Among the perquisites of holding public office are foreign travel opportunities not available to ordinary citizens.

In a series of three articles, the Valley News examines the practice of foreign governments picking up the tab for junketing local officials.

By JOHN MARELIUS and JOYCE PETERSON

Efforts by foreign governments to influence American public opinion extend well beyond Congress, all the way to Los Angeles City Hall.

Despite the South Korean influence-peddling scandal and a new political morality which supposedly frowns upon such things, the practice of junketeering by politicians is still thriving.

Right now, Los Angeles Mayor Tom Bradley and City Councilman Arthur Snyder are being wined and dined in the Orient on separate Taiwan junkets sponsored by Nationalist Chinese cities.

During the past two years, Snyder and Councilman John Ferraro have taken similar excursions to South Korea compliments of the Korean government.

State Department sources said the junkets are part of lavish public relations campaigns which both governments have been waging for years to generate support among Americans.

Invitations for such trips are extended to "every conceivable segment of opinion leaders" including elected officials, businessmen, educators and journalists, said a State Department official.

Mayor Bradley and his wife, Ethel, left Saturday, Sept. 3, for a three-week trip to include stops in Japan, Hong Kong and Taiwan.

Bradley's office said that while the air fare is being paid by the city of Taipei, the mayor will pay all other expenses out of his own pocket.

China Air Lines reported that the round-trip first-class fare for a flight to Japan, Hong Kong and Taiwan is $2,156 per person. Coach fare is $1,312.

Snyder's trip is being fully paid for by the People-to-People Fund of Kaohsiung, Taiwan's second largest city.

His mission is to present a wapiti, which is a western elk, to the zoo at Kaohsiung and a mule deer to the Taipei zoo. Both zoos are new and need animals and the Los Angeles zoo has a surplus of each.

While there, according to an aide to the councilman, Snyder will also be talking to business and industrial leaders about trade ties with Los Angeles.

Although Snyder's trip was arranged through the Chinese consulate in Los Angeles, there seems to be some mystery surrounding the People-to-People Fund which is picking up the tab.

Taiwan authorities in the State Department said they had never heard of the organization and I-nan Li, vice consul ofthe Los Angeles office, said, "We don't know anything about the People-to-People Fund."

Please turn to page 16, col. 1

Policeman hurt, manhunt on for hit-run driver

By MIKE POLLOCK

See photos, Section 1, page 18.

A manhunt was underway this morning for the driver of a car which collided with a Los Angeles police motor officer on the 6600 block of Lankershim Boulevard in North Hollywood Friday night.

The hit-and-run suspect, identified as Ignacio Ramirez of Arleta, fled from the scene of the crash on foot, police said.

The officer's gun was missing when he was found lying in the street, prompting police to believe the suspect took it.

Police identified the motor officer as Kenneth Williams of Canyon Country. He was in serious condition at St. Joseph Medical Center in Burbank with multiple fractures, lacerations and a concussion.

A passenger in the suspect hit-and-run vehicle, identified as Roberto Carrillo Chavira, 41, of Arleta, was taken to Serra Memor ial Hospital in Sun Valley with head injuries.

Witnesses said there were approximately 10 police cars and 15-20 motor officers looking for the suspect.

The search later expanded to include 100 officers from Valley Bureau Operations Task Force and all North Hollywood and Foothill Area officers.

The manhunt initially began in North Hollywood, but soon spread to the Arleta area.

The collision occurred at approximately 8:20 p.m. at 6623 Lankershim Blvd., in front of the El Tropicano Bar.

Police Lt. James Stirling said Williams was northbound on Lankershim Boulevard when a 1961 Pontiac Grand Prix made a left turn in front of him.

Williams struck the right side passenger door, breaking the window.

After the collision, the driver drove into the parking lot of the El Tropicano Bar. He then left the vehicle and fled on foot, police said.

This morning . . .

Following are occurrences of the past 24 hours, rounding out the news report compiled for Valley News readers this morning.

3-three-year-old starts killer fire

A 3-year-old girl playing with a cigarette lighter was believed the cause Friday of a Fontana house fire that killed a 22-year-old San Bernardino man.

The 3-year-old managed to escape the flames along with another child who were taken to safety by a young unidentified woman who lived at the house.

The body of Guillermo Fraga was found by firefighters in a hallway. He apparently had been overcome by smoke, authorities said.

Police said the young woman tried to use a garden hose to put the fire out, but flames engulfed the home.

Swim star puts talents to use

FREEPORT, Bahamas (UPI) — Faced with a stalled engine Friday, Olympic gold-medal swimmer John Naber had a ready solution — the American crawl to a nearby boat a quarter of a mile away.

But as luck would have it, that boat also had a stalled engine. So Naber, who won four gold medals and one silver in swimming at the 1976 Montreal Olympics, started kicking for shore a good mile away.

He landed at the Xanadu beach and told rescuers to hurry "because I hated to leave that guy out there all alone with three girls."

Rescuers were dispatched to tow in both the stalled boats.

Except for fog, it'll be fair day

Early morning low clouds and fog. Otherwise fair today through Sunday, with little change in temperature. Highs 85 to 92. Lows tonight mostly in middle 60s.

Tremors cause concern

Seismologists keeping close eye on Palmdale

By RICK ORLOV

Seismological studies are being stepped up in the Palmdale area because of swarms of mini-earthquakes during the past 10 months. Caltech scientists admitted to a growing concern at a Friday press conference.

Researcher Dr. Karen McNally said the public should not be alarmed by the small quakes, but should know of the seismic activity occurring along the San Andreas Fault.

Of concern to scientists, she said, is the fact the number of small earthquakes which has hit in the area since last November is highly unusual.

Also puzzling to researchers, she added, is the length of area affected by the tremors.

The earthquakes have registered between 0 and 3 on the Richter scale which measures intensity of ground movement. At this level, she said, most persons would not feel the earth moving.

One of the main things the scientists are looking at is whether the ground activity means a major earthquake is coming.

Two years before the February 1971 earthquake which hit the San Fernando Valley, she said, there was similar activity with swarms of minor earthquakes around the area which was the epicenter of the major temblor.

"We're not sure what it all means," Dr. McNally said. "But, we should be on our toes."

Another unusual feature of the earthquakes, she said, is the distance being affected by the ground movement.

When the small quakes began last November, she said, a six mile area was affected.

In May, the earthquakes stopped. Six weeks later, she added, the quakes returned and covered an area of about 20 miles.

Dr. McNally said, however, the small shocks may not mean anything.

"There have been a number of earthquakes where there were no foreshocks," she said. "We aren't making any predictions. The history of seismology in California is not really long enough."

Also, Dr. McNally said, researchers are not sure how the small quakes are related to the

Please turn to page 18, col. 4

Minimal spending asked

Supervisors back city bid for Olympics

By DAVE LINDORFF

A majority of the Los Angeles County Board of Supervisors supports the city's bid to host the 1984 Olympics, despite a warning by a top county financial analyst that the games would cost the county money.

Three supervisors, James Hayes, Peter Schabarum and Kenneth Hahn, strongly endorsed the city's bid this week in separate interviews, but they all added they wanted both city and county expenditures to be "minimal."

In addition, Supervisor Baxter Ward gave limited support to the city, but added, "If the city requires a financial partnership, the other party should be the state, with its present (budget) surplus, rather than the county, which necessarily must rely on the property tax."

The poll of top county elected officials came as a delegation of the U.S. Olympic Committee's site selection committee was preparing to visit here to examine the city's offer.

The delegation will be here today and Sunday and will view the facilities the city plans to use for the Olympics, including the Coliseum, which was originally constructed for the 10th Olympics, held here in 1932.

Perhaps more importantly, the delegation will question the city today about its Olympics budget proposal, according to John Argue, president of the Southern California Olympics Committee. "They will want to know how the city plans to pay for the games," he said.

According to Doug Steele, a county assistant administrative officer, that is also an issue that will have to be faced by county government.

Steele said no study has been conducted yet by the county, but explained, "There will undoubtedly be a financial impact." He said the county would "inevitably become involved in the area of crowd control and security, as well as roads and housing."

"As the chief law enforcement agency in the county, the Sheriff's Department would have to play a role," he said.

While all four supervisors contacted expressed concerns about the potential costs of the Olympic Games (Supervisor Ed Edelman is on vacation and unavailable for comment), none has apparently made the city formally aware of his views.

Supervisor Hayes explained his official silence on the issue, saying, "Up to this point, I don't think the city's application is far enough along for us to present an analysis."

Yet city officials have been debating cost estimates for some time. Mayor Tom Bradley's office has estimated that the city would have to spend about $33.5 million on construction to have all the necessary facilities for the games. His administrative assistant Anton Calleia has also predicted that operating expenses for the city would run as high as $150 million, but he claims that revenues generated would cover both capital improvement and operating costs.

On the other side of the argument, City Administrative Officer C. Erwin Piper has estimated that the city deficit from the games could range from $200.5 million to $336.5 million.

Any county costs would be in addition to this, and Steele said that "daily crowd control efforts" during the two-week Olympic Games "would inevitably dwarf the efforts we have at Rose Bowl time."

Moreover, it may be getting late for the county to influence the city's bid. A final decision on whether to select New York or Los Angeles as the U.S. site for the Olympics is expected to be made Sept. 25, when the U.S. Olympics Committee's executive board meets in Colorado Springs.

Supervisor Kenneth Hahn was the strongest county supporter of the city's bid to host the Olympics. As a member of the Coliseum Commission, he convinced that body to "enthusiastically endorse" the city's effort at a meeting last Wednesday. He also agreed when City Councilman Gilbert Lindsay, chairman of the commission, said he was "certain" the county would provide the sheriff's services during the games.

April 29, 1976

TEEN MARIJUANA USE RISING

Four of five Valley stations of the Los Angeles Police Department reported that more junior high school youngsters are smoking marijuana since penalties were modified.

Dec. 1, 1977

10 MURDERS LINKED TO SAME STRANGLERS

Los Angeles police Wednesday connected 10 murders of young women to the same stranglers as they conceded the killers may have posed as police officers. Three other murders since last September have not been tied by the LAPD's Hillside Strangler Task Force to the rash of killings

ABOVE: Water released from the Pacoima Dam turns Pacoima/Tujunga Wash into a raging river during a February 1978 rainstorm that eroded the backyards of homes on Tibbetts Street. Courtesy CSUN

Lakers Agree
To Magic Deal

EVER-GRINNING ALL-AMERICAN EARVIN "MAGIC" JOHNSON of Michigan State became the newest unofficial Laker Wednesday, agreeing with the NBA club to what was described by assistant general manager Chick Hearn as a "multi" contract.

The 6 ft. 8 inch, 200 pound sophomore guard, who average 17.1 points, 8.4 assists and 7.3 rebounds in 32 games last year, thus will forfeit his final pair of seasons in East Lansing in addition to a possible position on the 1980 U.S. Olympic team when he signs an NBA contract on or after June 25. That is the day the Lakers will inform the league office Johnson is the No. 1 pick in the NBA draft.

Feb. 14, 1979

SCHLESINGER, EXXON DIFFER ON $1 A GALLON GAS

Two powerful men - one a federal cabinet officer and the other the head of a powerful multinational oil company - differed markedly Tuesday on whether the price of a gasoline will rise to $1 gallon.

June 12, 1979

THE 'DUKE' IS DEAD

John Wayne, who so embodied the American hero in a half-century of movies that he became an internationally known symbol of the strong, patriotic American, died of cancer Monday. He was 72.

LEFT TOP: Actress and Honorary Mayor Beverly Garland, left, and Miss North Hollywood Liz Kasko, 1979. Courtesy The Weddington Family Collection

LEFT BOTTOM: Van Nuys Chamber of Commerce. Courtesy San Fernando Valley Historical Society

OPPOSITE: The Lakers' Magic Johnson and Kareem Abdul-Jabbar play the Seattle Sonics in a home game at the Forum. Daily News Archives

Sept. 7, 1979

WE'RE READY FOR THE BIG 7TH DAY; ARE YOU?

Only three days remain for the debut of the new Monday edition of the Valley News, an exciting package of news, features, sports and commentaries unlike any other seen in the San Fernando Valley.

Oct. 20, 1979

BIANCHI ADMITS 5 STRANGLE SLAYINGS; COUSIN ARRESTED

In a surprise move, Kenneth A. Bianchi Friday admitted killing five of the 13 Hillside Strangler victims and agreed to testify against his cousin, Angelo Buono, in 10 of the murders. A team of Los Angeles law enforcement agents immediately swooped in on Buono's Glendale home and auto upholstery shop and arrested the 45-year-old man on suspicion of murder, rape and kidnapping.

The 1980s & '90s

THE SOCIAL LANDSCAPE OF THE SAN FERNANDO VALLEY shifted in the 1980s as long-time residents moved to newer, more affluent communities and upwardly mobile minorities took their place. The Valley quickly evolved from a white suburban enclave into a melting pot of cultures, each with its own traditions and ideals, and each wanting a piece of the American dream.

In 1984, the Valley obtained its own area code – 818 – a signature that still serves to identify the other party as a "local" resident. A less complimentary identifier also took hold around that time – the Valley girl, a materialist teen with a distinctive speech pattern that was parodied around the country.

The region laid claim to two local heroes whose accomplishments took them to unimaginable heights. Astronaut Sally Ride of Encino became the first woman in space as a mission specialist on the shuttle Challenger in 1983. Two years later, Roger Mahony, who was raised on a poultry farm in North Hollywood, was named to oversee 4.5 Roman Catholics as archbishop of Los Angeles. He was elevated to cardinal in 1991.

The 1990s brought devastating news to thousands of workers in some of the region's most prominent industries. Facing sharp cuts in its federal defense contracts, Lockheed abandoned Burbank after more than 60 years and transferred operations to Georgia.

Hughes also closed its 1,900-worker Valley complex, while Litton Industries slashed its local workforce. General Motors, meanwhile, put 2,600 people out of work in 1992 when it closed the Van Nuys Assembly Plant – "Home of the Chevrolet Camaro and the Pontiac Firebird." Concern grew in the entertainment industry about "runaway production," as filmmakers moved to cheaper and friendlier venues for their shoots.

A traffic stop in Lake View Terrace in March 1991 evolved into one of the most shocking and violent incidents in Los Angeles history when an amateur photographer videotaped the beating of black motorist Rodney King by four white LAPD officers. Violence erupted after an all-white jury acquitted the officers of criminal charges. The six-day Los Angeles Riots left 53 people dead, thousands more injured and $1 billion in damage. The King beating and its aftermath forced the resignation of LAPD Chief Daryl Gates and an overhaul of the department's policies and procedures.

Just before 11 a.m. on Aug. 10, 1999, a white supremacist named Buford O. Furrow Jr. walked into the lobby of the North Valley Jewish Community Center and opened fire with a semiautomatic weapon, wounding five people. He then carjacked a motorist and drove to Chatsworth, where he murdered mail carrier Joseph Santos Ileto before surrendering to authorities. He eventually pleaded guilty to murder and weapons charges and was sentenced to life in prison. Although Furrow's message was one of hatred and vitriol, the incident ultimately served to bring together people of different colors and religions.

When it comes to natural disasters, Valley residents are well-acquainted with deadly flash floods and devastating wildfires. Yet the Northridge Earthquake on Jan. 17, 1994 is considered by many to be a defining moment in their lives. The 6.7-magnitude temblor hit at 4:31 a.m., flattening buildings, damaging freeways, sparking fires and killing nearly three dozen people. The powerful quake impacted communities as far away as Santa Monica and Fillmore, pushing damage estimates to nearly $25 billion and making it one of the nation's costliest and most destructive calamities.

As the 20th century ended, a group of Valley activists returned to an idea floated briefly in the 1970s – seceding from Los Angeles. They founded Valley VOTE (Voters Organized Toward Empowerment), with the mission of forming a more responsive and efficient government. They hoped the new millennium would provide the impetus for creating a new identity for Los Angeles' largest bedroom community.

— *Barbara Jones*

OPPOSITE: Crowds gather at the Sherman Oaks Street Fair on Ventura Boulevard to enjoy food, crafts and carnival rides in 1993. Courtesy Daily News Archives

RIGHT TOP: Chatsworth parade in the early 1980s.
Courtesy San Fernando Valley Historical Society

RIGHT BOTTOM: 10K run down Lankershim
Boulevard, from Universal Studios to the Television
Academy. Courtesy The Weddington Family Collection

June 10, 1980

RICHARD PRYOR CRITICALLY BURNED IN MISHAP

Actor-comedian Richard Pryor, 38, was
critically burned Monday right after a
cigarette lighter exploded in his face, setting
his clothes on fire, authorities reported.
Pryor was found in pain by Los Angeles city
firefighters after he collapsed on the street
in the 17200 block of Parthenia Street in
Northridge.

Nov. 5, 1980

REAGAN CRUSHES CARTER

Former California Gov. Ronald W. Reagan,
the ex-actor, passed the biggest screen test of
his life Tuesday, winning the presidency of
the United States by a margin even he could
not have imagined ... To the surprise of even
the most optimistic Reagan partisans, he
thrashed President Carter in the Democratic
strongholds of the Midwest and Northeast
and beat the president on his Southern home
turf.

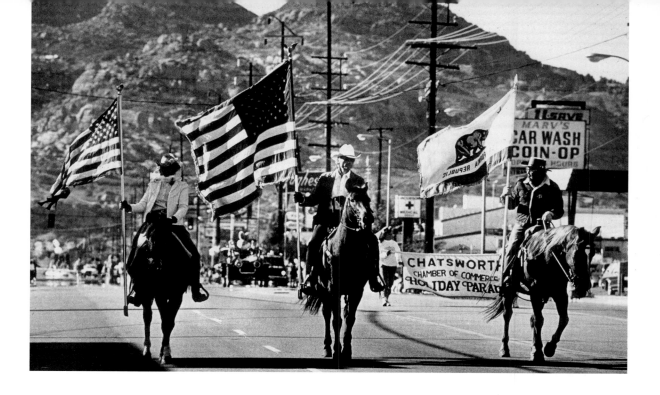

EXTRA EXTRA

Daily News

VOL. 70—NO. 148 | Monday, March 30, 1981 | 25c COPY

President Reagan shot; press aide is badly hurt

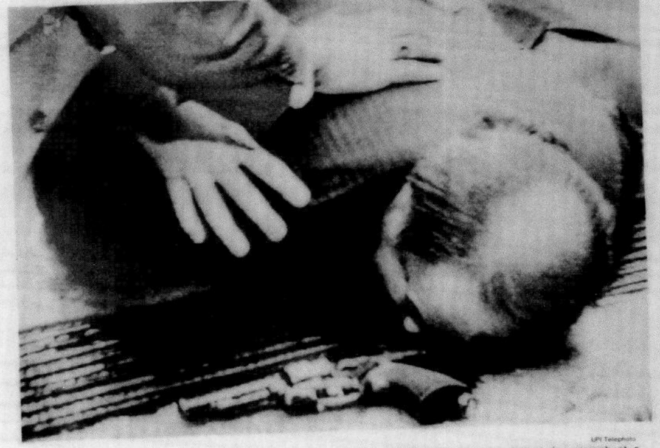

UPI Telephoto

White House press secretary James S. Brady lies wounded on sidewalk after a gunman fired several shots at President Reagan and his party after he delivered a speech at a Washington hotel. Brady was critically wounded.

By ROBERT BALLENGER
Daily News Staff Writer

President Reagan was shot once in the left chest in a close-range assassination attempt Monday outside a Washington hotel.

Press secretary James S. Brady was gravely wounded by a bullet in the head during the assassination try and was reported to be in very critical condition.

One of several bullets fired during the incident penetrated Reagan's body under his left arm, partially collapsing one lung but missing the president's heart.

Reagan was rushed to George Washington University Hospital where he was undergoing emergency exploratory surgery to locate the slug.

Also wounded in the shooting were Timothy J. McCarthy, a Secret Service Agent, and Thomas Delahanty, a Washington D.C. policeman, who was listed in critical condition.

The gunman, later identified as John Warnock Hinkley Jr., 22, of Evergreen, Colo., a community near Denver, opened fire with what was described as a .22 caliber handgun as Reagan stepped out of the hotel.

Hinkley's father, John W. Hinkley Sr., was later questioned at his home in Evergreen, Colo., by Secret Service agents.

The alert status of U.S. armed forces worldwide remained at normal peacetime readiness, dspite the shooting and wounding of the president, the pentagon said.

At least five shots were fired at the president from about 10 feet away as Reagan emerged from the Washington Hilton Hotel after addressing an AFL-CIO meeting.

The president, who had been waving to nearby spectators as he emerged from the hotel, turned in the direction of the shooting, but did not at first appear to have been struck by any of the bullets.

Secret Service agents escorting Reagan immediately hustled him into his limousine which then roared off.

One of Hinkley's shots struck the bulletproof window, leaving a pockmark but did not penetrate the glass.

Police and Secret Service agents pounced on the gunman, wrestling him to the ground and arresting him before carrying him over to a police squad car.

Sheriff's detectives in Golden, Colo., about 18 miles from Evergreen, said they have no information on whether Hinkley has a criminal record.

A check of Jefferson County Sheriff's Department records shows no listing for Hinkley, said detective Sgt. Donald E. Bennett.

"We'd never heard of him until we heard the report on the news and were called by the local FBI office to see if we had anything on him," Bennett said.

Reagan walked into the hospital, apparently unaware he had been wounded and that a bullet was lodged in his chest, presidential aide Lyn Nofziger told reporters.

"The president was holding his left chest with his arm, his head was bowed," said Willis King, a witness at the hospital when Reagan walked in. "There was blood on his shirt, his coat was opened . . . it was running down his shirt."

Nofziger told reporters the president was concious as he was wheeled into the operating room and making jokes.

Mrs. Reagan, who was not with her husband when he was shot, was whisked to the hospital to be at his side.

Please turn to page 4, col. 5

1 moment, Reagan smiled, then, gunshots and shock

By DEAN REYNOLDS
United Press International

WASHINGTON — President Reagan had just completed his speech, one of his many defenses of his economic program, when he headed to his waiting limousine.

Outside the Washington Hilton Hotel on Florida Avenue, the president was greeted by the cheers of several hundreds bystanders.

Reagan waved in his good-natured fashion and smiled to the crowd as he walked from a service entrance the 25 steps to the presidential limousine. As the president stepped off the curb onto the driveway where the vehicle was parked, something attracted his attention and he turned, facing the curb and the hotel wall where his assailant was standing somewhere among the bystanders.

Suddenly, there were four or five loud bursts, sounding like firecrackers, and the smell of gunsmoke hung in the air. The crowd recoiled in horror. People screamed. Handguns and automatic weapons were suddenly visible in the hands of police and Secret Service agents.

I dropped into a crouch but kept my eyes on the president. He appeared to have a frightened, almost bewildered look, just after the shots rang out.

Secret Secret agents spun him around and shoved him head first into the limousine, all the while the agents kept shouting "Get back! Get back!" to the crowd.

The shots, fired in rapid succession, could not have been fired from more than 10 or 15 feet from the president.

The limousine pulled away seconds after the president was pushed inside.

A scuffle to right of the limousine then caught my attention. A young, blond man was being subdued on the ground by several agents and policemen. There was a mob of lawmen on the ground and the tops of two legs, clad in dark trousers, were visible, sticking out from the pile.

I saw no one hit and learned only later the president had been wounded along with White House press secretary James S. Brady, two policemen and a Secret Service agent.

The gunman had been on the sidewalk, standing close to the hotel wall. Reporters were on the other side of the limousine, the top of a triangle from the president and the gunman.

It was like being in a vacuum, with everything in slow motion. It took a second or two before anything registered, but when I saw the looks of enormous stress and the clenched teeth of the Secret Service agents, I knew it was more than firecrackers.

I took off into the hotel to find a telephone, knocking down maybe eight persons who had just heard the president speak at the National Conference of the Building and Constructions Trade Department. There didn't seem to be a pay phone in the place, and I finally found an open telephone in an office.

When I got outside again, blood was mingling with the rain on the sidewalk.

Police roped off the area to hold back hundreds of curious pedestrians.

Across the street, I could see office workers watching on television the scene that had occurred just outside their windows.

Shooting shocks Reagan children

By KEN HOOVER
Daily News Staff Writer

Two of President Reagan's three children who live in California were reported in shock at news of the assassination attempt on their father.

The president's elder daughter, Maureen Reagan, 40, has been surrounded by Secret Service agents and moved to a "safe" location prior to flying to Washington, D.C., to be with her father, said a spokesman for KABC Radio, where she is employed as a talk-show host.

A spokesman for Patti Reagan Davis said she had no immediate announcement on her reaction or her plans.

Michael Reagan, 35, was in Burbank on business when he heard the news.

National and local political leaders today expressed shock and anger at the attempt to assassinate President Reagan.

Los Angeles County Supervisor Kenneth Hahn even called for beefed up security in the county Hall of Administration building in reaction to the shooting.

In Washington, Sen. Edward M. Kennedy, D-Mass., whose life has been touched twice by the assassination of his brothers, rose in the hushed chamber of the U.S. Senate to declare:

"I think all of us who care

Please turn to page 2, col. 5

EXTRA EXTRA

Daily News

SPECIAL EDITION

VOL. 70—NO. 192 | Wednesday, May 13, 1981 | 25c COPY

POPE SHOT

Pope has had big impact in his reign

Daily News Staff and Wire Services

The first non-Italian in almost five centuries as well as the youngest pope in more than 130 years, Polish Cardinal Karol Wojtyla was named Pope John Paul II in October, 1978.

In the summer of 1978 Pope Paul VI died and another Italian cardinal — Albino Luciani — ascended to the papal throne.

He paid honor to the two strong popes who had preceeded him and took the name — Pope John Paul I.

But 33 days later he too died and instead of following in the footsteps of John XXIII and Paul VI, he left behind only memories.

His death produced a political deadlock in the College of Cardinals that resulted in the ascension of Karol Wojtyla of Krakow to the papal throne.

When asked if he would accept the post, Wojtyla paused and said:"With obedience in faith to Christ, my Lord, and with trust in the Mother of Christ and of the Church, in spite of the great difficulties, I accept."

When asked what name he would take, he paused and then answered, "John Paul II."

In the 31 months since he became pope the man and the legend have become intertwined.

"He makes news in everything he does and seems to revel in it. The singing pope, the skiing pope, the swimming pope, the acting pope, the traveling pope," said an account written in 1979 in the Washington Post.

"He flouts tradition, he courts the crowds, he holds news conferences, he talks with reporters on his plane and in these things and many more conducts himself differently from any pope anyone has ever seen. He's a physical man who seeks a physical response and gets it," the report said.

He got the response when he became the first pope to be received at the White House in 1979 and to tour the United States. On that trip he also visited Des Moines, Ia., New York City, Philadelphia and Boston

As pope, John Paul II has underscored the church's traditional approach and beliefs.

Early in his reign he restated the church's longstanding rule of celibacy for priests despite the large numbers of priests who have been leaving the clergy.

He also let nuns know he did not approve of their wearing secular clothing in public, adding they should not permit feminist beliefs to overshadow their call to a chaste, poor and obedient life.

He has strongly stated the church's oppostion to abortion.

"You can't watch this man without being struck by his magnetism," said one account of his first year as pope.

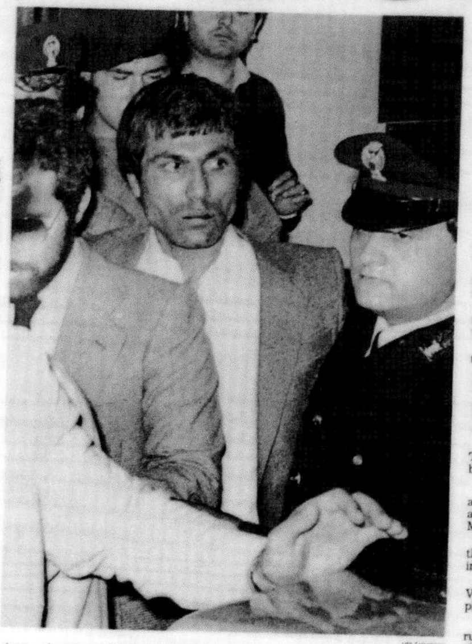

UPI Telephoto

A man, who was not identified, is taken into custody shortly after assassination attempt on Pope John Paul II. The man is being held in connection with the slaying attempt.

Political and church leaders are shocked

Church and political leaders expressed shock Wednesday over the shooting of Pope John Paul II and called for prayers for his recovery.

In Washington, D. C., President Reagan, himself the target of an assassin's bullet in late March, telephoned Terence Cardinal Cooke in New York City.

Acting White House press secretary Larry Speakes said the president "expressed shock and his words were, 'I'll pray for him.'"

Speakes said Reagan "expressed his personal concern and prayers for the pope."

Also in the nation's capital, State Department press secretary Dean Fischer said Secretary of State Alexander M. Haig Jr. was "shocked by the shooting" and was "following the situation very, very closely."

In Los Angeles, Timothy Cardinal Manning, archbishop of the Los Angeles dioscese, said it was "the generosity of the man" to allow himself to become part of the people, but the pontiff was "exposed to this violence" in the society.

Manning urged all churches to schedule masses to pray for the pontiff's recovery. A noon mass at St. Vibiana's Cathedral in downtown Los Angeles also was scheduled.

Mayor Tom Bradley said, "The pope is a man who has traveled the world as an emissary of peace, hope and goodwill. It saddens me to think of him as a target of such senseless violence."

The Polish ambassador to the United Nations, visibly shaken when informed of the shooting of the pope, said, "All the Polish nation will be shocked by this news and we will pray for his recovery."

Ryszard Frelek, in Nashville for a United Nations business council meeting, turned ashen when a reporter read a news service story about the shooting to him.

Before his election to the papacy, John Paul II was Karol Cardinal Wojtyla.

Gunman under arrest after attack in Rome

Daily News Staff and Wire Services

An unidentified gunman shot and gravely wounded Pope John Paul II today as the pontiff was riding in his open car through St. Peter's Square in Vatican City.

The pistol-wielding gunman, who was seized by authorities, fired several bullets at the pope, hitting him at least twice in the abdominal region.

Italian television said two women, one reportedly from New York, also were wounded during the shooting, one of them in critical conditon.

John Paul, 60, was rushed to a hospital in Rome where he underwent emergency surgery for bullet wounds near his pancreas.

The pope, who makes daily appearances in the historic square, had been standing in his open, jeep-like

Highlights of the pope's reign are pictured the back page.

car, greeting the crowd gathered there, lifting up babies, blessing bystanders and acknowledging cheers when the shots rang out.

Vatican security guards pounced on the gunman. There were conflicting reports as to his nationality, but officials said he was not Italian.

It was the first time a pope had been the object of an assassination attempt since a lone man disguised as a priest tried to stab the late Pope Paul VI at Manila airport during a trip to the Far East in 1970.

As John Paul was hit by the bullets, the impact of the gunshots knocked him sideways and he collapsed into the arms of two aides riding in the car with him.

The pope's driver then gunned the car through the Vatican's Arc of Bell inside the Vatican palace complex.

Within moments, an ambulance, its siren wailing, rushed into the palace. The wounded pope loaded aboard the emergency vehicle and it raced to Rome's Policlinico Gemelli Hospital where the surgery was performed.

Surgeons at the hospital operated on the pope for more than an hour, removing part of his small intestine that had been punctured by the bullet.

Doctors reported the pope received a blood transfusion but that no vital organs were damaged by the bullets and said the pontiff's condition remained grave.

As confusion over the incident subsided, thousands gathered in the square to pray along with a priest using the church's public address system. Many of those present fell to their knees and sobbed.

President Reagan, informed of the assassination attempt on the pope, expressed shock and, according to a press spokesman, said, "I'll pray for him.

Mayor Tom Bradley said he was "shocked and dismayed" at the news of the shooting.

"I wait anxiously, as does the rest of the world, for word on his condition," Bradley told City Hall reporters.

"The pope is a man who has travelled the world as an emissary of peace, hope and good will, and it saddens me to think of him as the target of senseless violence."

Vatican officals have often expressed muted fears the pope runs a great risk during his frequent forays into enthusiastic crowds that greet him wherever he goes.

April 4, 1981

FOR SANTA CLARITA VALLEY, A NEW DAILY NEWS

The Daily News is coming to the Santa Clarita Valley. Starting Monday, residents of this vibrant, growing area will be able to read a new edition of the Daily News ... Local news will be covered on our front page each day, and we'll have a specially designed section called the Santa Clarita Valley Daily News, where we'll explore events in depth.

June 9, 1982

LAKERS ON TOP OF WORLD

Jamaal Wilkes scored 27 points, and the Los Angeles Lakers shook loose from the stubborn Philadelphia 76ers Tuesday night for a 114-104 victory and their second NBA championship in the last three years. The Lakers' triumph came in the sixth game of the final series. Magic Johnson, who was the Most Valuable Player in the 1980 championship series when the Lakers also defeated the 76ers in six games, was voted the award again after his final game performance.

Aug. 15, 1982

SPREAD OF GANGS TO VALLEY

The Los Angeles County Grand Jury's final report
contains an ominous warning for the San Fernando
Valley. "Hispanic gangs are rapidly spreading into
the San Fernando Valley," the 1981-1982 report
concludes. Los Angeles police officers investigating
the rising tide of gang violence in the Valley agree
with that assessment. They note a steady escalation
of gang-related crime in the last several years.

June 14, 1983

'84 OLYMPICS TICKET SCRAMBLE UNDER WAY

The long wait for tickets to the 1984 Summer
Olympics is over. Beginning at 10 a.m. today, people
across the country will be able to pick up copies of
the official Olympic Ticket Information Brochure
and Order Form for tickets to the 1984 Summer
Games. The 32-page, full-color brochure and
order form will be available exclusively nationwide
through Sears, Roebuck and Co.'s 3,200 department
stores and catalog outlets.

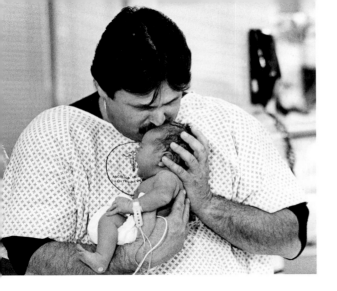

Jan. 23, 1984

RAIDERS ARE SIMPLY SUPER

The Los Angeles Raiders claimed the National Football League championship Sunday with a decisive 38-9 win over the Washington Redskins in Super Bowl XVII at Tampa Stadium. It was the widest margin of victory in the history of the Super Bowl.

Jan. 28, 1984

ROCK SUPERSTAR BURNED IN L.A. FILMING MISHAP

Grammy-nominee Michael Jackson, performing before about 3,000 people while filming a multimillion-dollar commercial in Los Angeles suffered second- and third-degree burns to his scalp Friday night after on-stage fireworks ignited his jacket and hair.

TOP LEFT: The first test-tube baby born in the San Fernando Valley cried a little, but turned quiet and content when his father gave him a kiss. Robert Anthony Brewer, son of a Los Angeles County firefighter and a computer saleswoman, was born at 8:05 a.m. on March 18, 1985 by Caesarean section, the first birth resulting from Northridge Hospital Medical Center's in-vitro fertilization program. Courtesy Daily News Archives

TOP RIGHT: The La Reina theater just before closing in 1985. Courtesy Joel Tator

LEFT: Civic Pride Committee members, from left, Chairman Cecil Pill, Donalda Towne and President Irwin Stanton clean the streets of Studio City in 1985. Courtesy Daily News Archives

Sept. 5, 1985

LOTTERY SALES TO START OCT. 3

California's long awaited lottery will begin at noon Oct. 3 when 400 million tickets go on sale for the first lottery game, Gov. George Deukmejian announced Wednesday. Deukmejian, who opposed the ballet measure creating the lottery and has vowed not to help publicize it, surprised reporters by joining lottery officials in announcing the long-delayed ticket sale.

June 15, 1987

TICKETS TO SEE POPE PREMIUM

Erika Hagin was standing in the refreshment line following Mass at Glendale's Holy Family Church on Sunday when she heard Monsignor Arthur Lirette call out her granddaughter's name. "Oh, my God," she exclaimed, turning to granddaughter Erika Anderson, a 17-year-old Glendale High School student. "We're going to the papal Mass!" ... Scenes such as these have been occurring throughout the three-county Roman Catholic Archdiocese of Los Angeles. Parishes have conducted lotteries to determine who will receive tickets to the two Masses that Pope John Paul II will celebrate during his September visit to Los Angeles.

L.A. throngs cheer pope

WITH A MESSAGE OF ENCOURAGEMENT FOR AMERICA'S YOUTH and a lecture for its top media leaders, Pope John Paul II swept into Los Angeles on Tuesday and was greeted by hundreds of thousands of people in the first papal visit ever to the nation's second-largest city.

On the streets of Koreatown and Little Tokyo, from the poverty of Skid Row to the gleaming towers of Universal City, the pope offered hope and demanded responsibility as he evoked an outpouring of faith from the country's largest Roman Catholic population.

At the end of his first day in Los Angeles, the pontiff celebrated Mass with more than 100,000 of the faithful at the Los Angeles Memorial Coliseum.

"California has been a symbol of hope and promise for millions of people who continue to come here to make a home for themselves and their families," the pope said in his 25-minute homily ...

Earlier in the day, the pope was given a rock star's welcome at Universal Studios, where he addressed 6,000 young Catholics and as many more watching by satellite from St. Louis, Denver and Portland, Ore.

The pontiff, who appeared more relaxed than at any earlier time on the tour, urged young people to have hope, and to find that hope in God.

"Why does it sometimes happen that a seemingly healthy person, successful in the eyes of the world, takes an overdose of sleeping pills and commits suicide?" the pope asked. "Why, on the other hand, do we see a seriously disabled person filled with great zest for life?

"The one has lost all hope," he said. "In the other, hope is alive and overflowing." ...

As he left, the pope said: "You are very good young people. What does it mean to be good young people? That you should be still better."

ABOVE: Pope John Paul II blesses Stephen Donley, 16, during a speech to 6,000 young Catholics at Universal Amphitheater. The pontiff, who was given a rock star's welcome, urged young people to have hope, and to find that hope in God.
Courtesy Daily News Archives

LEFT: City Councilman Joel Wachs, an AIDS activist, sits on a bus bench in Sepulveda that warns of the dangers of the disease. Courtesy Daily News Archives

BELOW LEFT: Snow blankets Braemar Country Club in Tarzana, February 1989.
Courtesy James R. Bozajian, Calabasas mayor

BELOW RIGHT: Rodney King calls for an end to the Los Angeles Riots on May 1, 1992. 'People, I just want to say, you know, can we all get along?' King said. The deadly riots were sparked by the acquittal of four Los Angeles police officers who were videotaped beating King after a traffic stop in Lake View Terrace on March 3, 1991. Courtesy Daily News Archives

Feb. 28, 1991

Bush declares gulf victory

A triumphant President Bush declared victory in the Persian Gulf war Wednesday night and announced that allied forces were suspending military operations until a permanent cease-fire could be arranged. "Kuwait is liberated. Iraq's army is defeated. Our military objectives are met," the president said in a dramatic televised address as the allies completed one of the swiftest routs in military history half a world away.

Oct. 27, 1992

Riding the rails

Lured by free fares and the prospect of headache-free travel, an estimated 5,300 commuters rode double-decker trains to Union Station on Monday as the Metrolink service ushered in a new era of commuter rail in Los Angeles. The 12 blue-and-white trains carried commuters, sightseers and dignitaries on three lines originating in Santa Clarita, Moorpark and Pomona - with all trains arriving within a few minutes of their scheduled times without any major hitches.

Sept. 4, 1993

Holdup suspect, 66, caught as she pedals from bank

A 66-year-old woman who was unable to withdraw her Social Security money to pay the rent pulled out a handgun and robbed a bank of $242 on Friday, according to police, who said they arrested the woman as she pedaled away on her bicycle ... Bank employees told police the woman came into the bank and asked a teller if her Supplemental Social Security check had been automatically deposited into her account. The teller told her that the check had not been deposited, and that no funds were available to withdraw from her account. Police said the woman responded by pulling a pistol from her purse, pointing it at the teller and saying: "Now can I have my money?" ... The teller counted out $242 for the woman, who then walked calmly out of the bank and climbed onto her bicycle, according to a police report.

LEFT: A firefighter attaches a winch to a car that was pushed several feet by water from a broken pipeline under Coldwater Canyon Avenue in September 1993. Courtesy Daily News Archives

OPPOSITE: Rocketdyne workers in Canoga Park assemble a post-boost vehicle for the nation's Peacekeeper missile program, 1993. Courtesy Daily News Archives

BELOW LEFT: Emergency workers treat Steve Longsinger, a 29-year-old dispatcher who was shot and wounded by a disgruntled coworker at Homedco in Glendale, Sept. 2, 1993. Another employee died in the shooting. Courtesy Daily News Archives

BELOW RIGHT: Glendale firefighters battle a 15-acre brush fire that drew near some homes before it was brought under control in September of 1993.
Courtesy Daily News Archives

ABOVE: Sherman Oaks and Hazeltine in the aftermath of the 1994 earthquake. Courtesy Michael Smith

BELOW: The Northridge Earthquake forces a gas main to explode. Courtesy Jim Ridosh

June 14, 1994

SIMPSON'S EX-WIFE SLAIN

Hours after his former wife and an acquaintance were found slain outside her luxury town house, former NFL star O.J. Simpson was questioned Monday by police who searched his nearby estate to gather evidence in the case ... A police source said a blood-stained glove was found at Simpson's Brentwood estate, about two miles from the crime scene, and that it matched a glove found near the bodies.

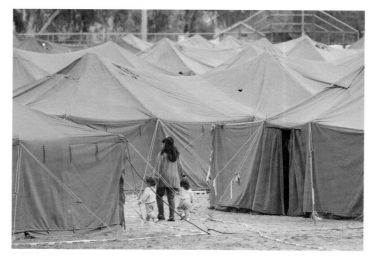

ABOVE: The city of Fillmore in Ventura County was hit hard by the quake. Among the damaged buildings was the Fillmore Hotel.
Courtesy Daily News Archives

LEFT: A woman leads two children through a maze of tents set up by the National Guard for displaced quake victims at Lanark Park.
Courtesy Daily News Archives

Aug. 26, 1994

A BIG LITTLE LEAGUE WIN

Under a gray, gloomy sky, with thunder booming in the distance, a band of 14 Northridge Little Leaguers dubbed "The Earthquake Kids" made history Thursday. Ace pitcher Nathaniel Dunlap threw a one-hitter and outfielder Spencer Gordon hit a three-run home run to help Northridge defeat Springfield, Va., 3-0, to win the U.S. championship at the Little League World Series before a crowd of 20,000 at Howard J. Lamade Stadium. Northridge will play for the world championship Saturday afternoon against Maracaibo, Venezuela.

TOP LEFT: David Teraoka, a member of the U.S. champion Northridge Little League team, shakes hands with former President Reagan in Century City, 1994. Courtesy Daily News Archives

TOP RIGHT: Arleta residents continued a 26-year battle in 1994 for the return of their former ZIP code, 91332. Courtesy Daily News Archives

155

June 24, 1995

RAIDERS COMMIT TO OAKLAND

Raiders owner and NFL maverick Al Davis agreed Friday to abandon Los Angeles and take his team back to Oakland, ending 13 years of feuding, fighting and sometimes winning in Southern California. The move would leave Los Angeles without a professional football team for the first time since 1945 ... Poor attendance during his years in Los Angeles weighed against the fervor in Oakland over the team's return also played roles.

Sept. 4, 1996

DAILY NEWS, AOL CREATE ON-LINE SITE

In a partnership aimed at forming a vibrant local on-line community in Los Angeles, the Daily News has launched a site on America Online as part of AOL's new Digital City Los Angeles.

TOP: LAPD officers and SWAT team members use a commandeered armored transport to rescue a wounded man, under fire from a robber at the Bank of America across the street, February 28, 1997.
Photo by Gene Blevins/Los Angeles Daily News

RIGHT: Bystanders huddle under a police cruiser, caught in the cross-fire of a gun battle between LAPD officers and heavily armed bank robbers.
Photo by Gene Blevins/Los Angeles Daily News

FAR RIGHT: Clad in body armor and armed with high-powered weapons, one of the two robbery suspects takes aim at police.
Photo by Gene Blevins/Los Angeles Daily News

Oct. 18, 1997

PACIFIC BELL HIKING PRICE OF PAY PHONE CALL

The cost of a local call on a Pacific Bell pay telephone will increase to 35 cents beginning Monday, the company has announced. The 15-cent hike is the first in California since 1984 ... Directory assistance information, which had been free of charge from area pay phones, will soon cost 35 cents after technological modifications are made.

March 28, 1998

THERAPIST ADMITS TO 40-50 MERCY KILLINGS

A respiratory therapist who said he viewed himself as an "angel of death" has confessed to killing between 40 and 50 patients over an eight-year period at Glendale Adventist Medical Center, authorities said Friday. Efren Saldivar, a Tujunga resident, reportedly made his confession March 11 to Glendale police, who interrogated him after getting an anonymous tip.

ABOVE: A couple leaves a triage clinic at Granada Hills Community Hospital on Jan. 17, 1994, hours after the Northridge Earthquake hit.
Courtesy Daily News Archives

LEFT: 'Tail O' the Pup' hot dog stand, originated in San Fernando Valley and moved to West Los Angeles, 1999. Courtesy Brett Yollis

June 5, 1998

ELWAY COMES HOME

When John Elway walked the halls of
Granada Hills High School in the late 1970s,
he was a big man on campus — leading the
baseball team to back-to-back city cham-
pionships and the football team to the city
playoffs. On Thursday, he was the biggest
man on campus. The 37-year-old Denver
Broncos quarterback and Super Bowl champion returned to Granada Hills to join 3,500
fans for the renaming of the football field as
John Elway Stadium ... After the ceremony,
the quarterback was mobbed by students,
and fans in orange and blue Bronco jerseys.
He was given flowers, and after kissing a
woman's cheek, she wandered through
the throng with her hands on her cheeks,
screaming, "Oh, my God. Oh, my God. He
kissed me. Oh, my God."

RIGHT: Built by MCA and Texaco, the 36-story
Universal City Plaza is the tallest building in the San
Fernando Valley. Courtesy The Weddington Family Collection

158

ABOVE: City Councilman John Ferraro, third from left, at a ground-breaking ceremony for a Ralph's supermarket. Courtesy The Weddington Family Collection

Jan. 10, 1999

VALLEY'S NET GAIN

San Fernando Valley residents will be the first in Los Angeles to step into an Internet revolution this year, with the debut of online access through cable television lines at speeds 100 times faster than the telephone links common in most homes. The breakthrough will finally open the door for innovations that companies and futurists have long promised: Video on demand, instant music for fans and the ability for graphic artists, architects, engineers, musicians and others to work from home just as easily as they would from their office or studio, according to Internet experts ... The service, called Road Runner, will be available come summer to Time-Warner Communications' 120,000 customers in the West Valley and surrounding areas.

Oct. 22, 1999

400 STUDENTS JOIN MELEE AT GRANT HIGH

A melee between about 400 Armenian and Latino students erupted at Ulysses S. Grant High School on Thursday, injuring 14 students and two teachers in a frenzy of fistfights and thrown trash cans, officials said. Administrators said the fight grew out of a long-simmering ethnic feud on the Oxnard Avenue campus adjacent to Los Angeles Valley College.

A New Millennium

THE FIRST DECADE OF THE 21ST CENTURY WAS A TIME OF upheaval for the San Fernando Valley, the state and the nation. While the horror of the 9/11 terror attacks was felt by every American, local residents also found themselves shaken, touched and influenced by events close to home.

Minutes after reporting mechanical problems, an Alaska Airlines jet bound from Mexico to Seattle plunged nose-first into the Pacific Ocean off Point Mugu. A total of 88 passengers and crew died in the crash on January 31, 2000.

James Hahn, scion to a family political tradition, defeated Antonio Villaraigosa in June 2001 to become mayor of Los Angeles. Four years later, Villaraigosa unseated Hahn and became the city's first Latino mayor since 1872.

Cries of "celebrity justice" went up as "Baretta" star Robert Blake was acquitted of murdering his wife outside Vitello's restaurant in Studio City. Bonnie Lee Bakley, the mother of the couple's young daughter, was shot in the head while Blake went back inside the restaurant to retrieve a handgun. Although Blake was found not guilty in a criminal trial, a civil jury found him liable for her wrongful death.

The family and friends of Daniel Pearl created a foundation and a music festival in honor of the slain Wall Street Journal reporter, who grew up in Encino and graduated from Birmingham High School. Pearl was kidnapped Jan. 23, 2002, and killed by Al-Qaeda while working on a story in Pakistan. A high school in Van Nuys also bears his name.

In the November 2002 election on Valley secession, cityhood won by a narrow margin locally but was defeated 2-to-1 by voters across Los Angeles. Had the campaign succeeded, the name of the new city would have been San Fernando Valley, California.

After a 10-year grass-roots campaign against the development of Ahmanson Ranch, community leaders celebrated the purchase of the 2,900-acre expanse in eastern Ventura County to be preserved as open space. The state paid $150 million in October 2003 to buy the land from Washington Mutual and make it part of the Santa Monica Mountains Conservancy.

The political shock waves that shook California in October 2003 were akin to the Big One, with the recall of Governor Gray Davis and the election of Arnold Schwarzenegger to replace him. The body builder-turned-action star trounced the Davis, whose low-key personality put him at a distinct disadvantage when compared with the charismatic Austrian.

The Valley mourned victims of not one but two Metrolink crashes — the horror magnified by the cause of the separate tragedies. In January 2005, an SUV abandoned on the railroad tracks near Glendale in an aborted suicide attempt set off a spectacular three-train collision that left 11 dead and more than 180 injured. The man responsible for the crash was convicted of murder and sentenced to life in prison.

Then, on September 12, 2008, a Metrolink engineer sending a cell-phone text message to a teen-age fan missed a red light, putting the commuter train into the path of an oncoming freight train. The engineer and two dozen passengers were killed and more than 100 others were hurt. A $200 million settlement paid by the contractor who employed the engineer was divided among victims' families and survivors.

A decade-long plan to build a Children's Museum in Lake View Terrace imploded in 2009, as the recession, weak public support and funding problems forced officials to file for bankruptcy.

The mortgage meltdown that spread into a global economic crisis started in the Valley's own backyard. Calabasas-based Countrywide Financial Corp. topped a list of 25 lenders responsible for extending subprime mortgages to homeowners who might not otherwise have qualified for a mortgage.

Finally, in a sign of the how times have changed, the Valley Fair was forced to drastically scale back operations after failing to find a home for its livestock show. The event that in its heyday drew some 60,000 fans will instead be limited to 4-H contests and agriculture education — a nod to the industry that supported the local economy for so many years and provided the base for the growth of the San Fernando Valley.

— *Barbara Jones*

OPPOSITE: Arturo Montiel, 19, and his 14-year-old brother, Giancarlo, play basketball at Sun Valley Park. Photo by Hans Gutknecht/Los Angeles Daily News

Feb. 26, 2000

PEREZ SENTENCED TO FIVE YEARS

Remorseful for betraying his badge, his city and his family, former LAPD Officer Rafael Perez was sentenced Friday to five years in prison under a plea bargain deal he received for revealing a police corruption scandal that has rocked Los Angeles' criminal justice system. Dressed in blue prison garb and shackled with handcuffs chained to his waist, Perez spoke haltingly in court, detailing his gradual slide into corruption that included shooting, beating and framing innocent victims.

LAKERS NBA **EXTRA!**

LOS ANGELES

Daily News

Online: dailynews.com   MONDAY, JUNE 19, 2000   25 Cents

L.A. CHAMPS!

Lakers beat Pacers in 6 games for NBA title

Online: dailynews.com   THURSDAY, SEPTEMBER 13, 2001   50 Cents
DESIGNATED AREAS HIGHER

ATTACK ON AMERICAN SOIL

TERROR

Spencer Platt/Getty Images

An explosion rocks the World Trade Center this morning after terrorists crashed two airplanes into the twin 110-story towers in New York City. Death tolls are expected to climb into the thousands.

Hijacked planes wipe out World Trade Center, damage Pentagon and shatter American security

By Jerry Schwartz
Associated Press

NEW YORK — In one of the most horrifying attacks ever against the United States, terrorists crashed two Los Angeles-bound airliners into the World Trade Center in a deadly series of blows today that brought down the twin 110-story towers. A plane also slammed into the Pentagon as the government itself came under attack.

Thousands could be dead or injured, a high-ranking New York City police official said, speaking on condition of anonymity.

Authorities had been trying to evacuate those who work in the twin towers when the glass-and-steel skyscrapers came down in

But the airline later said that was unconfirmed. Two United airliners with a total of 110 aboard also crashed — one outside Pittsburgh, the other in a location not immediately identified. Altogether, the planes had 266 people aboard.

"This is perhaps the most audacious terrorist attack that's ever taken place in the world," said Chris Yates, an aviation expert at Jane's Transport in London. "It takes a logistics operation from the terror group involved that is second to none. Only a very small handful of terror groups is on that list. ... I would name at the top of the list Osama bin Laden."

President Bush ordered a full-scale investigation to "hunt down the folks who committed

People flee from the collapse of the World Trade Center this morning as terrorists leveled both of the twin towers. Another commercial airliner crashed into the Pentagon as the United States fell under attack.

Suzanne Plunkett
Associated Press

Birth brings light to dark day for family

DANIEL JOHN LEE MADE HIS LIVING ON THE ROAD — A SUPER-vising carpenter on tour with the Backstreet Boys.

Friends said the touring made for a tough life — he was away from his wife, their child and their Van Nuys home often. But family held its place in his priorities, so he boarded American Airlines Flight 11 on Tuesday in Boston headed to Los Angeles to participate in the birth of his second child.

"He didn't make it," his wife, Kellie Lee, said Thursday, resting in Encino-Tarzana Regional Medical Center, holding newborn Allison Danielle ...

Kellie Lee, 32, sat surrounded by congratulatory flowers and balloons, holding her 8-pound, 11-ounce newborn on what should have been a hallmark day for the family.

"I have a hard time being happy," she said, "but I am glad (Allison) is here." ...

Los Angeles County residents and people who worked in the county are among the victims who have been identified as being on flights that terrorists hijacked and crashed. Among them are:

Producer David Angell, 54, one of the co-creators of the acclaimed NBC sitcom "Frasier," and his wife, Lynn, were returning from a Cape Cod wedding, friends and family said.

Berry Berenson, widow of "Psycho" star Anthony Perkins and younger sister of New York-based model-turned-actress Marisa Berenson, was on her way home from a Cape Cod vacation.

Edmund Glazer, 41, the chief financial officer and vice president of finance and administration for Chatsworth-based MRV Communications Inc., who was traveling from his Boston-area home on company business.

Thomas Pecorelli, 31, of Topanga Canyon was a cameraman for Fox Sports and E! Entertainment Television. He was returning home to his pregnant wife ...

Dr. Yeneneh Betru, 35, of Burbank was a re-nowned doctor of internal medicine who practiced at a number of local hospitals. Betru was on his way home from Ethiopia after a two-week visit with his family ...

Dora Menchaca, 45, of Santa Monica was director of medical affairs at Thousand Oaks-based Amgen and had been in Washington to meet with Food and Drug Administration officials about a prostrate cancer drug.

She was scheduled on a later flight but changed her travel plans so she could spend more time with her family

LEFT: Kellie Lee holds her newborn baby Allison Lee on Thursday, two days after her husband Dan Lee died when American Flight #11 from Boston to Los Angeles crashed into the World Trade Center. Lee gave birth to her second child at the Encino-Tarzana Regional Medical Center. Two year-old Amanda Lee gives her mom a balloon at right. Photo by Charlotte Schmid-Maybach/Los Angeles Daily News

Nov. 29, 2001

SHAQ FOR SHERIFF?

He's got a $200 police uniform, custom fitted. A polished Sam Browne belt. Size-22EEE policeman's boots. He's short only the gun, badge and nameplate. "O'Neal." Shaquille O'Neal, towering chairman of the court for the Los Angeles Lakers, may soon be the big gun of the Los Angeles Port Police Reserves. The 7-foot-1, 340-pound center who has commanded NBA hoops for nearly a decade is being specially trained in the San Fernando Valley by Los Angeles County sheriff's deputies for harbor patrol duty. His ultimate goal: Shaq for sheriff. "I just have a love for policemen because they've always been the real heroes in my life," the superstar center said during a recent locker-room interview. "I would like to have a leadership role."

Feb. 22, 2002

LOSS HITS ESPECIALLY HARD IN VALLEY WHERE HE GREW UP

The family and friends of Danny Pearl vowed Thursday that The Wall Street Journal reporter will live on in the powerful legacy of a man who grew up in the San Fernando Valley and went on to pursue truth in the midst of terrorism — at the cost of his life. With the confirmation of Pearl's death, family and friends wept tears of sorrow and anger, then testified to the reporter's enduring mark on the world. For Pearl's family, including parents Judea and Ruth, who live in Encino, and his two sisters, the grief was deeply personal. They released a statement calling their only son their "walking sunshine of truth, humor, friendship and compassion." ... Pearl was kidnapped Jan. 23, while working on a story about a possible link between shoe-bomb suspect Richard Reid and the al-Qaida terrorist network.

LEFT: Ron England of Granada Hills, left, and Make-a-Wish recipient Caleb Clark, 11, feed the last $100 worth of England's million-penny collection into a CoinMaster machine at Pavilions market in Burbank. Photo by Gus Ruelas/Los Angeles Daily News

FAR LEFT: Don Larson circulates voting materials during the Old Northridge Neighborhood Council election. Courtesy Linda Dunham

OPPOSITE TOP: 'I never thought I would see this day,' said Ernestine Reyes on learning that her nephew, Ritchie Valens, would be inducted into the Rock and Roll Hall of Fame, March 2001. Here, Reyes holds a portrait of Valens in her Pacoima home. Photo by Charlotte Schmid-Maybach/Los Angeles Daily News

OPPOSITE BOTTOM: Judea Pearl, father of slain journalist Daniel Pearl, talks with visitors at Daniel Pearl Music Day in Encino Park, October 6, 2002. Photo by Phil McCarten/Los Angeles Daily News

ABOVE: Myra Ferrant of Tarzana, left, and Jodell Hays of Studio City watch secession vote returns in Sherman Oaks, November 5, 2002. The majority of Valley residents voted to secede, but the measure was defeated.
Photo by Tina Burch/Los Angeles Daily News

Aug. 7, 2002

ARTS CENTER FOR VALLEY

Los Angeles County supervisors voted unanimously Tuesday to put a $250 million bond issue on the Nov. 5 ballot that would help fund a $75 million, 1,600-seat performing arts center at California State University, Northridge ... At CSUN, the bond measure would raise $15 million for fire and earthquake safety measures in the San Fernando Valley's largest performance hall. The remaining $60 million would come from a $15 million private sector match and other funding sources, officials say. CSUN President Jolene Koester called the venue, proposed for the northwest corner of East University Drive and Nordhoff Street, a "natural" for the university.

165

Encino woman makes mail call less lonely for military forces

EVERY SOLDIER, SAILOR, AIRMAN AND MARINE WILL TELL YOU the same thing: The highlight of any day is mail call. The half-hour or so you gather around, waiting to hear your name called.

When you get a letter or package from home, you can't wait to rip it open. When you don't, you walk away in a funk.

And when you never get that letter or package, you don't even bother showing up for mail call anymore.

The company commanders and platoon sergeants in the Middle East right now know who's not getting those packages from home. That's why some of them have been e-mailing Carolyn Blashek.

They give this Encino woman the names of the men and women in their companies who could use a lift right about now — the GIs who seldom or never hear their name at mail call.

"Carolyn, I received a package from your Operation Gratitude, and would really like to express how much I appreciate it. It is the first package I have received.

"I was wondering if you could add another soldier to the list. He is a single soldier, and hasn't received mail yet. Thanks again, SPC K.S. in Iraq."

… And that's how Operation Gratitude was born, with a big lift from local businesses and groups that helped Carolyn early on by donating items to fill those packages, and local school kids who wrote thank you letters to put in them.

April 30, 2003

101 FIX SCALED BACK

Rejecting a controversial plan to double-deck the Ventura Freeway through the San Fernando Valley, transportation officials on Tuesday recommended widening the freeway between Thousand Oaks and Burbank and adding regular traffic and car-pool lanes. They also said widening the freeway to accommodate two car-pool lanes in each direction would allow flexibility for express buses or even a rail line in the future, and give those who carpool direct connections to the 405 and 134 freeways.

May 20, 2004

'HOT' WATER AT SANTA SUSANA

High levels of radioactivity were found for the first time in groundwater at the Santa Susana Field Lab where nuclear reactors were tested beginning in the late 1940s, federal officials said Wednesday. Officials said the contamination does not pose a risk to the public or neighbors of the facility located in the Simi Hills above Chatsworth … The Daily News first disclosed in 1989 that a DOE survey had found massive radioactive and chemical contamination at the lab, triggering the effort.

And away we go! MTA launches the busway with great hoopla

ABOVE: Governor Arnold Schwarzenegger chats with a student in music class during a tour of the consistently high-performing Vaughn Next Century Learning Center in Pacoima, January 28, 2005. Photo by John McCoy/Los Angeles Daily News

ABOVE RIGHT: Passengers ride the Orange Line during the opening day of the 14-mile-long busway, October 29, 2005. Photo by Andy Holzman/Los Angeles Daily News

IN THIS CAR-CRAZED REGION, CROWDS OF PEOPLE WAITED IN line Saturday under the San Fernando Valley sun to do the unthinkable — ride a bus.

The Metro Orange Line debuted to more than 30,000 curious passengers, many of whom stood for up to an hour in a line snaking around a city block to try the long-awaited mass transit line across the Valley.

On board the silver double-length buses, some found an alternative to grueling freeway commutes. Others saw a way to get around on weekends. And others found nothing worthwhile to draw them back.

"We think it's a wonderful idea whose time has come," said Calabasas attorney Jerry Posell, on board with his wife, Ellen, on a practice run for a potential trip downtown ...

The Valley has waited more than 20 years for an east-west transit line that was promised when vot-ers first approved new taxes for transportation. The busway wasn't the Valley's first choice but emerged as a compromise when it became clear the MTA had no money left to build a subway or light rail. Its total cost was $350 million ... The Orange Line promises a 40-mile ride across the Valley, about as fast as the freeway during rush hour...

The morning saw Mayor Antonio Villaraigosa and Supervisor Zev Yaroslavsky out greeting riders, while later on Councilman Tom LaBonge was on hand and Councilwoman Wendy Greuel brought her toddler out for a look. MTA officials, who rolled out more buses to meet the crowd, were thrilled with the turnout.

"I couldn't have asked for a better start," said Yaroslavsky. "This is what I predicted from Day One. Let people vote with their feet."

Aug. 14, 2006

VINELAND BOYS ABOUT TO FACE JUDGMENT DAY

They had gone by boyish names like Sneaky, Big Barney, Little Joe and Yuck. But federal charges filed against 49 defendants linked to the notorious Vineland Boys street gang involve anything but kid stuff: Cop killing. Witness slaying. Racketeering. Conspiracy. A 78-count criminal felony indictment also includes numerous drug and firearms charges against the east San Fernando Valley gang members… One law enforcement official called it the largest street-gang case in memory.

L.A. GALAXY LANDS SOCCER STAR IN $250 MILLION DEAL

The city of stars woke up to a supernova January 11 — the world's most famous soccer star had signed on to play for the Los Angeles Galaxy in the richest deal in sports history. The estimated $250 million, five-year pact with David Beckham marked the biggest Los Angeles sports deal since hockey legend Wayne Gretzky joined the Kings nearly two decades ago. With his wife, Victoria — formerly Posh of the Spice Girls pop group — Beckham joins the elite of L.A.'s celebrity culture.

ABOVE: Courtney McCanon and other competitors in the girls 10-and-under 200-meter freestyle take to the water at the Santa Clarita Aquatic Center. Photo by David Crane/Los Angeles Daily News

RIGHT: Local residents check in at the Leonis Adobe Museum for the premiere of a documentary about the Calabasas landmark, November 3, 2007. Photo by Tom Mendoza/Los Angeles Daily News

OPPOSITE TOP: George Barris is an icon of car customizing in the Valley. His creations include the Batmobile and hundreds of other cars featured in movies and TV shows. Photo by David Sprague/Los Angeles Daily News

OPPOSITE BOTTOM LEFT: A photograph taken with a fisheye lens distorts the image of Bruno, a 9-month-old chihuahua, whose owners are enjoying a visit to the Griffith Observatory, December 29, 2007. Photo by John Lazar/Los Angeles Daily News

OPPOSITE BOTTOM RIGHT: A curious pug pokes around the Thousand Oaks Pug Meetup Group that gathers monthly at the Conejo Creek Dog Park, February 2008. Photo by Evan Yee/Los Angeles Daily News

Sept. 24, 2008

FORECAST: THE STATE COULD GO INTO A NOSE DIVE BECAUSE OF CRISIS, EXPERTS SAY

After predicting for the past four years that California will be able to avoid a downturn, UCLA economists now say the state may plunge into recession because of the ongoing financial crisis. "Worst-case, we can go into a real deep recession," said David Shulman, senior economist at the university's Anderson Forecast.

Oct. 14, 2008

FIRESTORM: 10,000 ACRES ALREADY TORCHED

Two Santa Ana wind-driven fires on opposite ends of the San Fernando Valley raged out of control Monday night, destroying dozens of homes, forcing the evacuation of thousands of residents and threatening to charge all the way to the ocean. At least two deaths were blamed on the blazes, which some 800 firefighters were battling on steep canyon hillsides from the Northeast Valley to Rocky Peak. The Sesnon Fire, which started shortly after 10:30 a.m. on Oat Mountain northeast of Porter Ranch and had burned more than 5,000 acres to the west by late Monday, came on the heels of Sunday's Marek Fire.

ABOVE: The Beatles tribute band Ticket to Ride draws fans to Warner Center Park, July 20, 2008.
Photo by John Lazar/Los Angeles Daily News

BELOW: Father Anthony Rasch at Saint Mary the Virgin Anglican Rite Church in Chatsworth, May 6, 2008.
Photo by Hans Gutknecht/Los Angeles Daily News

ABOVE: Members of Cub Scout Pack 118 from Northridge wave to the crowd during the Granada Hills Holiday Parade, December 7, 2008. The annual parade features a variety of holiday-themed floats and local marching bands. Photo by David Crane/Los Angeles Daily News

LEFT: Snow flies as Jason Myerson, front, and Kyle Hoyt, both 7, sled down a hill at Chatsworth Hills Academy, where 30 tons of man-made snow turn the campus into a winter wonderland, December 12, 2008. Photo by Michael Owen Baker/Los Angeles Daily News

Nov. 16, 2008

DEVASTATION

With 600 households, well-manicured lawns and luxury amenities, Oakridge Mobile Home Park was no trailer park. The gated community, most of which was reduced to ash by a roaring wildfire that swept through the Sylmar hills late Friday and early Saturday, featured a putting green, an Olympic-size swimming pool and tennis courts ... Fire officials estimate that up to 500 of the park's mobile homes were destroyed - making the Sayre Fire among the single-most destructive fires in terms of home loss in the Los Angeles area in nearly half a century.

LEFT: Petra Bides holding original Pumpkin Festival poster in Calabasas, 2009. *Courtesy Arlene Bernholtz*

BOTTOM LEFT: Everardo Galvez of Yorba Linda draws the image of artist Frida Kahlo on a Sherman Way sidewalk during a 2008 Day of the Dead festival in Canoga Park. *Photo by David Crane/Los Angeles Daily News*

BOTTOM RIGHT: Van Gogh Elementary second-graders Rachel Nakkoud, left, and Christina Valiquette react to a performance of 'The Nutcracker Suite,' December 18, 2008. The girls, dressed as Chinese dancers, were also part of the show. *Photo by Tina Burch/Los Angeles Daily News*

ABOVE: Gay Goodwin on her horse Barrybrown and Paris Tanaka astride Spud ride through Cheeseboro Canyon in Agoura Hills, January 3, 2009. Photo by Michael Owen Baker/Los Angeles Daily News

LEFT: Kids enjoy the giant slide in the carnival section of the California Poppy Festival at Lancaster City Park in 2009.
Photo by Jeff Goldwater/Los Angeles Daily News

BELOW: Shoppers buy fresh produce from the ONEGeneration Farmers Market held Sundays in Encino.
Photo by Andy Holzman/Los Angeles Daily News

July 17, 2009

A HERO'S WELCOME

After an exhausting and sometimes harrowing 13 months at sea, 17-year-old Zac Sunderland of Thousand Oaks sailed home to a hero's welcome, capturing the record for the youngest person to circumnavigate the globe solo. With a large American flag unfurled behind his 36-foot vessel, Intrepid, Sunderland sailed into history at 10:30 a.m. as he completed a 28,000-mile voyage with two world records - one of which will never be broken. He became the first person under the age of 18 to circumnavigate the world, as well as the youngest ever to do so.

Nov. 4, 2009

BECK GETS THE CALL

Deputy Chief Charlie Beck, a 33-year Los Angeles Police Department veteran with "LAPD blue" in his blood, was picked by Mayor Antonio Villaraigosa to head the department — ending weeks of speculation about who would fill the big shoes left by William Bratton. The mayor's choice, widely cheered by rank-and-file officers, the police union and civil rights groups, was expected to sail through the City Council over the next two weeks.

ABOVE: Motorists on the 23 Freeway get a close-up view of snow dusting the Santa Monica Mountains, February 18, 2009.
Photo by Tina Burch/Los Angeles Daily News

LEFT: The 55,000-square-foot Roy and Patricia Disney Family Center Center opens in Spring 2010 at Providence Saint Joseph Medical Center in Burbank. The $36 million outpatient center features state-of-the-art equipment, a patient research center, spiritual and psychological counseling and a healing garden. Photo by Andy Holzman/Los Angeles Daily News

OPPOSITE TOP: The band Blue Lagoon performs classic jazz at Casey's Tavern in Canoga Park. With live music and a ban on swearing, the bar draws patrons both young and old. Photo by David Crane/Los Angeles Daily News

OPPOSITE BOTTOM: People watch a preview during a tour of the Muvico Theaters at The Oaks Shopping Center in Thousand Oaks, February 17, 2009. Photo by Michael Owen Baker/Los Angeles Daily News

ABOVE: Visitors enjoy a sunny afternoon at CityWalk at Universal Studios, June 26,2009.
Photo by Andy Holzman/Los Angeles Daily News

LEFT: Skateboarders try out the new Santa Clarita Skate Park during its grand opening. March 27, 2009. Photo by Evan Yee/Los Angeles Daily News

RIGHT: Julie Crouch watches Karen Young putt the ball at Scholl Canyon Golf Course, built atop a former landfill in Glendale, April 17, 2009. Photo by John McCoy/Los Angeles Daily News

March 12, 2010

COCKFIGHTING RING BUSTED BY AUTHORITIES

Breaking up what police call one of the largest cockfighting rings in Los Angeles history, investigators raided two Sylmar properties housing some 2,200 steroid-fueled birds that fought with metal blades in two covered arenas. The birds were so aggressive that they injured several investigators during the Wednesday morning raid.

Dec. 22, 2010

VALLEY'S GROWTH BRINGS CHANGES

Average San Fernando Valley residents are smarter than they were a decade ago, but they're also spending more of their paychecks on mortgages and speaking less English at home, according to U.S. Census data released Tuesday. More than 1.7 million people now make up the Valley, a population that now exceeds all U.S. cities except New York, Los Angeles, Chicago and Houston ... The Valley's population grew just 4.7 percent from 2000 to 2009, far less than the state's population growth of 10 percent. California grew at its slowest pace since 1910.

ABOVE: Connor Doyle and Landon Lopez dress as 'Luxord' and 'Zexion' for the Anime Expo at the Los Angeles Convention Center, July 2, 2010. Thousands of Japanese animation fans donned costumes, wigs and makeup for North America's largest anime and manga event. Photo by Andy Holzman/Los Angeles Daily News

BELOW: Rides are just part of the fun at the 2010 California Strawberry Festival in Oxnard. The weekend festival boasts music, carnival games, handicrafts and an endless variety of strawberry confections. Photo by John McCoy/Los Angeles Daily News

ABOVE: Butchers prepare for the grand opening of Whole Foods Market's flagship store in Tarzana, May 2010. The 50,000-square-foot store anchors Tarzana Village Walk, a mixed-use project being developed at Ventura Boulevard and Yolanda Avenue. Photo by Michael Owen Baker/Los Angeles Daily News

LEFT: A California black bear cub tumbles to the ground after being shot with a tranquilizer gun, May 26, 2010. The cub had wandered down from the foothills and climbed a pine tree in a Porter Ranch neighborhood. It is released back into the wild. Photo by Gene Blevins/Los Angeles Daily News

ABOVE: Fans seek autographs from their favorite players before the start of the 2010 Major League Baseball All-Star Game in Anaheim, July 13, 2010.
Photo by Andy Holzman/Los Angeles Daily News

LEFT: Los Angeles Lakers star Kobe Bryant celebrates as his team clinches the NBA championship. The Lakers defeat the Boston Celtics, 83-79, in Game 7 on June 16, 2010. Photo by John McCoy/Los Angeles Daily News

BELOW: The three-story Media Arts Center at Mission College in Sylmar is slated to open in late 2011. The 51,600-square-foot building features classrooms, a production studio, an editing lab and an art gallery.
Photo by Michael Owen Baker/Los Angeles Daily News

January 30, 2011

MISSION COLLEGE CULINARY ARTS
DEDICATED TO SERVING UP SUCCESS

The student chefs worked side by side in a choreographed frenzy, fixing a gourmet meal fit for a queen, or a president. But there was one special ingredient at the Culinary Arts Institute at Los Angeles Mission College that distinguished its award-winning cuisine. "We show our students the love for the art of food," said founding Executive Chef Rudy Garcia. "The love for it. The feel for it. The taste for it. "The love." The culinary institute, founded 20 years ago in a fledgling home economics kitchen on the Sylmar campus, has become a national food preparation leader. And it's poised to become a foodie powerhouse. For two years running, its students have won a national bistro championship, besting chefs from culinary arts schools across the country and those of the U.S. armed services ... The northeast San Fernando Valley institute has just hired a faculty chef from Le Cordon Bleu who previously served U.S. presidents at Camp David and the White House. And in February, Mission College will open a $45 million LEEDS Platinum center — containing no fewer than seven distinctive kitchens — to be renamed the Institute of Culinary Arts.

ABOVE: The choir at Woodland Hills Community Church commemorates the 50th anniversary of Dr. Martin Luther King Jr.'s visit to their church. King preached at two services on January 15, 1961, then spoke to at a community forum at Canoga Park High School. Photo by Dean Musgrove/Los Angeles Daily News

LEFT: Hikers make their way up a trail at Topanga State Park, one of many scenic spots that entice visitors to the rustic canyon community, January 2011. Photo by John McCoy/Los Angeles Daily News

March 11, 2011

FUNICELLO'S HOUSE BURNS

Annette Funicello, the Disney Mouseketeer who later starred in a series of beach-party movies, suffered smoke inhalation in a fire that gutted her Encino home. Funicello, 68, who suffers from multiple sclerosis, was taken by ambulance to a local hospital after she and two other people — identified by neighbors as husband Glen Holt and a nurse — fled the burning home. Although the fire was concentrated in the rear and attic of the 3,600-square-foot home, officials said the structure and its contents were badly damaged by smoke, heat and water. The interior of the house appeared charred, although passers-by could see posters from some of Funicello's movies and performances mounted on the wall of the two-car garage. Funicello became a household name in 1955, when she was hand-picked by Walt Disney to be one of the Mouseketeers on his new television variety show, "The Mickey Mouse Club."

ABOVE: Six years after its debut, the Orange Line busway remains a popular transit option for San Fernando Valley commuters.
Photo by Andy Holzman/Los Angeles Daily News

LEFT: The $125 million Performing Arts Center opens in January 2011 at California State University, Northridge. The 1,700-seat facility is built with state-of-the-art acoustics and energy-saving features.
Photo by David Crane/Los Angeles Daily News

ABOVE: Foliage frames the high-rise office buildings in Warner Center in this view from the Topanga overlook, February 9, 2011. Photo by Andy Holzman/Los Angeles Daily News

Galpin Motors

ESTABLISHED 1946

Galpin Motors, owned and operated by Bert and Jane Boeckmann and their family, is one of the San Fernando Valley's most compelling and enduring business success stories, beginning in the City of San Fernando in 1946...

FRANK GALPIN OPENS GALPIN FORD ON FEB. 25, 1946, IN THE CITY OF SAN FERNANDO. THE SHOWROOM HOLDS THREE VEHICLES.

BERT BOECKMANN JOINS GALPIN FORD IN 1953 AS A SALESMAN, BECOMES GENERAL MANAGER IN 1957, VICE PRESIDENT IN 1960, PRESIDENT IN 1964, AND SOLE OWNER/PRESIDENT IN 1968.

ALWAYS LOOKING FOR THE NEXT AUTOMOTIVE INNOVATION, BERT TEAMS WITH HEINZ PRECHTER TO INTRODUCE EUROPEAN SUNROOF TECHNOLOGY TO AMERICA. THE U.S. SUNROOF INDUSTRY IS BORN!

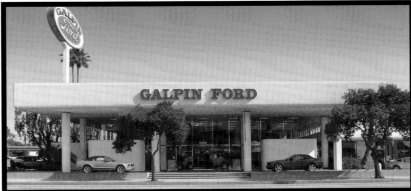

GALPIN FORD MOVES TO ITS CURRENT LOCATION AT 15505 ROSCOE BL., NORTH HILLS/ VAN NUYS, IN 1966. THE NEW SHOWROOM FEATURES DISPLAY SPACE FOR 17 VEHICLES. BERT'S VISIONARY THINKING FOR THE NEW GALPIN FORD DEALERSHIP INCLUDES A FULL-SERVICE RESTAURANT ADJACENT TO GALPIN FORD. THE POPULAR HORSELESS CARRIAGE RESTAURANT QUICKLY BECOMES A VALLEY FAVORITE FOR BREAKFAST, LUNCH AND DINNER. IT IS THE FIRST IN-DEALERSHIP RESTAURANT IN AUTOMOTIVE HISTORY.

GALPIN MOTORS | 15505 ROSCOE BLVD., NORTH HILLS, CA 91343 | (800) GO-GALPIN | WWW.GALPIN.COM

Galpin Motors

ESTABLISHED 1946

"GALPIN SQUARE" – WITH THE DAZZLING FORD DEALERSHIP, RESTAURANT, FREE COMMUNITY MEETING FACILITIES AND VAST OPEN AREAS SUITABLE FOR PROMOTIONS AND ENTERTAINMENT -- BECOMES AN IDEAL "COMMUNITY CENTER" FOR FAMILY EVENTS.

ONE OF GALPIN FORD'S EARLY SPONSORSHIPS IN THE COMMUNITY INCLUDES THE GALPIN SKY DIVING CLUB, WHICH SETS A WORLD RECORD IN 1977 FOR PERFORMING A 10-MAN STAR JUMP.

BERT REDEFINES THE CUSTOMIZING BUSINESS IN THE 60S, AND GALPINIZED® VEHICLES MAKE GLOBAL HEADLINES AND DRAW ATTENTION ON THE ROAD EVER SINCE! BERT AND JANE'S SON, BEAU, GALPIN VICE PRESIDENT, TAKES "GALPINIZING" TO NEW HEIGHTS WITH GALPIN AUTO SPORTS (G.A.S.), WHICH OPENS IN 2006.

MAYOR TOM BRADLEY CONGRATULATES JANE AND BERT BOECKMANN WHEN GALPIN FORD WINS THE BRAND NAMES FOUNDATION AUTOMOTIVE RETAILER OF THE YEAR AWARD IN 1969 AND AGAIN IN 1974.

GALPIN MOTORS | 15505 ROSCOE BLVD., NORTH HILLS, CA 91343 | (800) GO-GALPIN | WWW.GALPIN.COM

Galpin Motors

ESTABLISHED 1946

THE BOECKMANN FAMILY LAUNCHES GALPIN JAGUAR IN 1999 WITH THE WORLD PREMIERE OF THE XK8. JAY LENO IS ON HAND TO TAKE DELIVERY OF THE VERY FIRST JAG XK8.

THE BOECKMANN FAMILY, ALWAYS EMPHASIZING GOOD CITIZENSHIP IN THE COMMUNITY, SUPPORTS COUNTLESS EDUCATIONAL, CULTURAL, SPIRITUAL, POLITICAL AND SERVICE ORGANIZATIONS AROUND THE WORLD. THEY INSTILL THIS SPIRIT IN THEIR GALPIN FAMILY AS WELL - ENCOURAGING EMPLOYEE INVOLVEMENT IN THE COMMUNITY. GALPIN OFTEN HOSTS EVENTS SUCH AS BLOOD DRIVES, COLLECTING SCHOOL SUPPLIES AND HOLIDAY TOYS.

CLUB ASTON OPENS IN 2005, IMMEDIATELY ACCLAIMED AS THE MOST UNIQUE ASTON MARTIN SHOWROOM IN THE WORLD. A LARGE CONTINGENT OF ENTERTAINMENT, POLITICAL AND SOCIETY CELEBRITIES ATTENDED THE GALA GRAND OPENING.

WITH THE VISION AND LEADERSHIP OF BERT, JANE AND THEIR FAMILY, GALPIN MOTORS HAS EXPANDED THROUGHOUT THE DECADES TO INCLUDE 10 AUTOMOTIVE FRANCHISES - FORD, LINCOLN, SUBARU, HONDA, MAZDA, VOLVO, JAGUAR, LOTUS, ASTON MARTIN AND SPYKER. AS WELL AS GALPIN PUBLIC AND STUDIO RENTALS, GALPIN AUTO SPORTS, AND GALPIN STARBUCKS.

GALPIN MOTORS | 15505 ROSCOE BLVD., NORTH HILLS, CA 91343 | (800) GO-GALPIN | WWW.GALPIN.COM

Van Nuys Airport

ESTABLISHED 1928

THE VAN NUYS AIRPORT OPENED AS THE METROPOLITAN AIRPORT ON DECEMBER 17, 1928 - THE 25TH ANNIVERSARY OF THE WRIGHT BROTHERS' FIRST SUSTAINED, POWERED FLIGHT

Although it is famous for its role as the setting for airport scenes in the Bogie-Bergman classic "Casablanca" and for years was known as the busiest general aviation airport in the world (a distinction it still attains at times), the more important claim to fame for Van Nuys Airport (VNY) is its profound impact on Southern California.

Every year, VNY contributes more than $1.3 billion to the region's economy, supports more than 12,300 jobs, and generates an earnings impact of more than $704 million – without depending on local tax dollars. It's financed entirely by revenues from lease, rental, and user fees. Far from using tax dollars, it adds to state and local tax revenues to the tune of nearly $80 million annually.

It also plays a major, if unsung, role in greatly reducing congestion and flight delays at regional commercial airports such as Los Angeles International (LAX), thanks to over 380,000 take-offs and landings each year of private, corporate, charter, military, fire, police, air ambulance, search-and-rescue, and news media aircraft.

The airport was the brainchild of a corporation formed by a small group of citizens, and opened as the Metropolitan Airport on Dec. 17, 1928 – the 25th anniversary of the Wright Brothers' first sustained, powered flight. The airport took up about 80 acres amid farmland in the then-rural San Fernando Valley. Many famous aviation pioneers were regulars there, including Howard Hughes, who used it as the site for scenes in his ambitious 1930 World War I aviation epic, "Hells Angels."

According to a 2006 Los Angeles Times article, Amelia Earhart flew out of the airport in November of 1929 to set a speed record of 184 mph – and less than a year later, Pancho Barnes, one of Hollywood's first female stunt pilots – took off from one of its runways to break that record, flying 196.19 mph.

Although the Great Depression hit the airport hard, by 1941 it had revived to become the biggest, busiest general aviation airport in America. At the start of WWII, the U.S. government bought the airport and converted it into a military base, adding 163 acres for an Army airfield and using it to train P-38 Lightning pilots, among other things.

VAN NUYS AIRPORT I 16461 SHERMAN WAY, VAN NUYS CA 91406 I (818) 442-6500 I WWW.LAWA.ORG

Van Nuys Airport

ESTABLISHED 1928

After the war, the City of Los Angeles bought the airport for a token $1, agreeing to let the California Air National Guard operate at the site. By now, the airport covered 400 acres; its name was changed to San Fernando Valley Airport. Soon, the airport became so prosperous that the companies operating on its grounds were generating an annual payroll total of $43 million. In 1957, the airport's name was changed to Van Nuys Airport.

In the '60s, the airport became home to many aerospace companies, even as land around it filled up with homes. Eager to work with surrounding communities, VNY did such things as establish the FlyAway Bus Terminal, which provides non-stop bus service between the Valley and LAX and helps relieve freeway and LAX parking congestion. It also implemented a Noise Abatement and Curfew Ordinance to minimize negative impacts of airport operations on neighboring homes.

The California Air National Guard relocated to a different airport in 1990; the area it had used became the operation site for the American Red Cross when it gave aid to victims of the 1994 Northridge Earthquake.

VNY, LAX, Ontario International Airport, and Palmdale Regional Airport are owned by Los Angeles World Airports (LAWA), whose airport systems are directed by a policy-making board of Airport Commissioners appointed by the Mayor of Los Angeles. In 2006, the Mayor signed VNY's master plan for a $15 million residential soundproofing program. Shortly afterward, a $30 million bond project by the L.A. Fire Department began construction of permanent air operations and helicopter maintenance facilities at VNY's former Air National Guard site.

Today, the airport's 730 acres are home to more than 100 businesses including five fixed-base operators providing aircraft storage and parking, aviation fuel, aircraft sales, flight instruction, aircraft charters, and aircraft maintenance. VNY serves as home to such famous aircraft as the seasonal Super Scoopers that fight southland wildfires. TV and radio helicopters utilize VNY to help reporters deliver up-to-the-minute traffic and news reports.

Throughout the changes in its 80-plus years, VNY held its starpower as an economic powerhouse as well as

VAN NUYS AIRPORT IS FAMOUS FOR ITS ROLE AS THE SETTING FOR AIRPORT SCENES IN THE BOGIE-BERGMAN FILM CLASSIC "CASABLANCA"

a setting for scenes in countless movies and TV shows. It is poised to continue having star roles in Southern California's economy as well as many movie classics yet to be filmed.

VAN NUYS AIRPORT | 16461 SHERMAN WAY, VAN NUYS CA 91406 | (818) 442-6500 | WWW.LAWA.ORG

Red Barn Feed and Saddlery

ESTABLISHED 1954

There were a lot of horses in the Valley in the mid 1950s, so the then-new Red Barn Feed and Saddlery did fine by focusing almost exclusively on equestrian-related needs. But by the time retiring Cal State L.A. teacher Phil Carter bought the store in 1985, things had changed so that when he first began, while the store itself was huge, its product appeal and customer range was so narrow as to make working there a bit boring.

"I thought, 'There has to be more than this,'" he recalls. He embarked on an intense six-week research jag, investigating every other pet store in the Valley, meeting with product vendors, and absorbing everything he could about local pet-owner demographics. He realized that in order to make the kind of store people needed most, it would have to have superior quality food at the lowest prices possible, and a staff that knew exactly what they were doing when it came to helping customers with their pets.

For a beginning business owner – Carter bought the store because he realized he'd reached the point where he was teaching the kids of former students, which he took as a sure sign it was time for him to move on – he showed remarkable savvy. Today, there are four Red

Barn stores (the original Tarzana store; Red Barn Feed Too, in West Hills; Red Barn Also, in Granada Hills, and Red Barn Pet Express in North Hollywood). All of them demonstrably have a larger selection of higher quality products at lower prices than even the most recognizably-branded national discount pet stores.

Yet Carter doesn't take credit, except in that because he can buy in large volume and doesn't have to deal with a cumbersome corporate hierarchy, the stores are extremely nimble and competitive. Instead, he gives much of the credit to Red Barn employees, many of whom have worked there as long as he has. Their commitment to the proper care and feeding of every kind of pet is more than a job – it's a passion.

"But most of all, the stores are really made by customers who care about their pets," he says. "To come to this kind of store, you have to take an extra step. Our customers have special dedication to their pets."

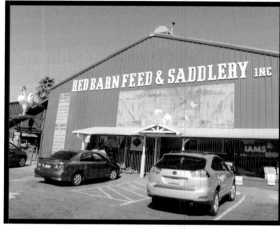

RED BARN FEED, THE ORIGINAL TARZANA STORE

OUR STAFF

THE BARN

RED BARN
FEED & PET

RED BARN FEED | FOUR LOCATIONS IN THE VALLEY | (818) 345-2510 | REDBARNFEEDANDPET.COM

Hamer Toyota

ESTABLISHED 1965

Cars broke down frequently in 1917, including in the area then surrounded by orange groves where Sepulveda and San Fernando Mission boulevards intersect. For

1965, HAMER TOYOTA, SEPULVEDA BOULEVARD & SAN FERNANDO MISSION BOULEVARD

drivers it was like being stuck in the middle of nowhere. Fortunately for them, Lee Hamer, whose father had just bought some of those orange groves, was mechanically minded and kind of heart; he'd usually stop work on his dad's farm long enough to help change a tire, fill a radiator, or make a quick repair.

In 1939, Hamer bought the property from his father and opened a gas station where servicing cars was as important as selling gas. Soon, Hamer was selling cars and servicing them, too. Over the next two-plus decades, he held more than 40 auto franchises, selling nearly every

kind of American, European, and Asian import imaginable, from Hudsons to Fiats. His business philosophy was iron-clad: If you give customers a good deal, they might come back, but if you give them a good deal and great service, they'll always come back.

In 1965, he shocked everyone by dropping all the franchises and becoming the nation's first exclusive Toyota dealership. Most people thought he was crazy – Americans then were skeptical of Japanese cars. But Hamer saw in the little Toyota a solid, reliable automobile that was easy to service, and service in his book was one of two keys to a successful dealership.

The other key was trustworthiness. At the time, car salesmen had a reputation for being unscrupulous. Hamer had zero tolerance for shady practices, and came down hard on any employee he thought was being untruthful with customers.

His dealership became known for honesty and good service. People trusted Hamer, including his judgment in cars, and his Toyotas sold well. By the time he died in 1995, his dealership was one of the most highly awarded in the industry. He was very respected by the community for his quiet but extremely generous support of local charities.

Hamer Toyota, owned by Donald Redding and the Hamer family since Lee Hamer's death, is still on the original property. Many of its workers have been there for upward of 30 years. Now in its fourth generation of customers ~ some have bought literally dozens of cars from Hamer – service and ethics remain its guiding principles.

TODAY, HAMER TOYOTA & SCION, SEPULVEDA BOULEVARD & SAN FERNANDO MISSION BOULEVARD

HAMER TOYOTA | 11041 SEPULVEDA BLVD., MISSION HILLS, CA 91345 | (818) 365-9621 | WWW.HAMERTOYOTA.COM

189

Valley Presbyterian Hospital

ESTABLISHED 1958

Most people don't remember what medical care was like in the Valley before Valley Presbyterian Hospital opened in 1958. Many folks in need of hospital attention had to go "over the hill" into Los Angeles proper to get it. VPH was one of the Valley's first full-service hospitals, a distinction signifying a tradition of "firsts" that started before it even opened and which has continued for more than 50 years.

PHASE ONE GROUNDBREAKING CEREMONY FOR THE FIRST 63-BED UNIT OF THE FUTURE VALLEY PRESBYTERIAN HOSPITAL

VPH's beginnings couldn't have been more auspicious. The first circular hospital in the world, it was honored by Modern Hospital Magazine for design excellence even before it officially opened. The design was revolutionary: it had no dead-end corridors, every patient room had a view, and it reduced the number of steps nurses had to make by more than a third. It was renowned as a model for hospitals around the world.

Back then, VPH had 63 beds. It has since grown into one of the Valley's largest and most prestigious independent non-profit hospitals, with 350 beds and more than 500 physicians representing virtually every specialty and most sub-specialties.

In 1965, it was the site of the first open-heart surgery in the Valley, pioneering the Valley's first open heart surgery program. Five years later, it was the first Valley hospital to open an intensive care neonatal nursery. The first quintuplets born in California were delivered at VPH in 1971.

In 1977, it was the first in the Valley to open a dedicated oncology unit. The Valley's first coronary angioplasty was performed at VPH in 1981. Five years later, it opened the first private Labor-Delivery-Recovery hospital rooms in Southern California with its groundbreaking Women's and Children's Center. A year later,

CHILDREN WHO WERE BORN AT VPH DIG FOR ONE OF THE 50 DOLLAR-FILLED PIGGY BANKS BURIED AT THE PHASE THREE CONSTRUCTION SITE

ON THE EAST SIDE OF VPH IS THE SITE OF THE SEVEN-STORY CIRCULAR TOWER — PHASE THREE INCLUDED AN ADDITIONAL 180-BEDS AND PLANS FOR A PEDIATRICS DEPARTMENT, OUTPATIENT CLINIC, HEALTH LECTURE HALL, CHAPEL AND MORE

in 1987, it opened the Valley's first Pediatric Intensive Care Unit, treating young patients from up to 175 miles away. In 1992, its cardiologists ranked among the top in the nation, with a coronary angioplasty success rate in the 94th percentile range.

VPH's tradition of excellence continues to extend to nearly every area of medicine. Valley residents clearly value VPH's place in the Valley's past and in its future, voting it "Best Medical Center" every year in readers' polls for the past six consecutive years.

VALLEY PRESBYTERIAN HOSPITAL | 15107 VANOWEN STREET, VAN NUYS, CA 91405 | (818) 782-6600 | WWW.VALLEYPRES.ORG

Horace Heidt Estates

ESTABLISHED 1960

In 1939, a Hollywood producer asked New York City's famous big band leader Horace Heidt to come to Southern California to make the movie "Pot O' Gold." Heidt knew he'd be bringing with him 30 musicians and their families, so he bought an orange grove property in Sherman Oaks with plans to put them up in style while they were here.

HORACE HEIDT ESTATES

Thus began a unique piece of living history that could only happen in the San Fernando Valley: Horace Heidt Estates. For more than 50 years, people have loved living at this resort-style rental community so rich in Hollywood mystique that it has continuously served as a backdrop in hundreds of TV shows and movies, all the way up to a "CSI: Crime Scene Investigation" shot

Magnolia Estates
Apartment Homes

Haleakala
New Luxury Apartment Homes

on location there just last month.

Heidt's quest to provide classy lodgings for his band evolved into a home sanctuary for all manner of industry professionals. By the late 1950s, The Estates had 45 elegant apartment units, multiple swimming pools, and an 18-hole golf course, all in the classic Palm Springs resort style that epitomized '60's "cool." Heidt soon added an equally chic Hawaiian Village with 115 apartments, a ballroom, and ten stand-alone houses, each with a pool. The grounds also included his own home, recording studio, and production office.

HORACE HEIDT'S BOOK IS AVAILABLE
AT HORACEHEIDTSTARMAKER.COM

Resident musicians, singers, and actors made it a lively if respectable place filled with parties nearly every weekend. Heidt was known throughout his career as an

upright, generous man; thousands grieved when he died in 1986. By then, Heidt's son, Horace Heidt Jr., had taken over the Estates. In 2006, he added the Haleakala Apartments to the property.

HORACE HEIDT ESTATES - ORIGINAL ARTISTS' RENDERING

Many celebrities have lived at Horace Heidt Estates – Dick Van Patton, Ed Begley Sr. and Jr., Bob Cummings, Barbara McNair, Roberta Sherwood, Barbara Hale, Joey Heatherton, and Marilyn King of the legendary King Sisters, to name a few.

Heidt Jr. spent ten years researching and writing a stunning book called "Horace Heidt, Big Band Starmaker," published last year. A treasure for anyone interested in the history of the San Fernando Valley, it is filled with original photographs and fascinating insight on Horace Heidt, the Estates, Big Band music, and more, with a CD of music plus a DVD of historic film footage to supplement its pages. The book is now available at www.HoraceHeidtStarmaker.com.

HORACE HEIDT ESTATES | 14155 MAGNOLIA BLVD., SHERMAN OAKS CA 91423 | (818) 784-8211 | WWW.HORACEHEIDTESTATES.COM

Community Chevrolet

ESTABLISHED 1959

Most auto dealerships bear the name of the owner, as was the case when Lou Bell and partner Roger Sorensen bought a car dealership in Burbank in 1959. Instead of renaming the dealership after themselves, the two agreed to give it a name in keeping with their vision of the role the business would play in the lives of its neighbors and customers, whom Bell viewed as interchangeable.

"In a way, the name my grandfather chose, 'Community Chevrolet,' was a statement of his business philosophy," says Fred Bell Jr., who now owns the dealership with his sister, Business Manager Jana Dean. "He viewed this business as not just selling cars, but building lasting relationships with customers. Part of building those relationships was giving back to the community as a whole, supporting things like youth programs and education. My grandfather envisioned Community Chevrolet as a hub for the community. That's how it's been for three generations."

Lou's son, Fred Bell Sr., got involved in the business at a young age, and by the early '60s, also had his own dealership in Tujunga, Fred Bell Chevrolet. In 1981, Community Chevrolet moved from the corner of First Street and Olive Avenue to its current location about a block away.

As a boy, Fred Jr. worked at Community Chevrolet, doing everything from washing cars to parking them in the service lane. He later worked his way up through various departments to learn the business. Meanwhile, his sister, Jana Dean, helped at the business office at the Tujunga dealership.

ORIGINAL LOCATION 1ST & OLIVE-1970

"My father didn't push us into the auto industry," Fred Jr. recalls, "but he was very good at providing us the right education, such as sending me to the dealer academy training program. He was always trying to move us along in the right direction."

Fred Jr. and Jana Dean worked for other auto dealerships to gain broader perspective. Both ended up coming back to Community Chevrolet; when Fred Sr. died early this year, the two took over the company. It is the last remaining new car dealership in Burbank. Fred Jr. says a lot of things have changed since it first opened 52 years ago, but the dealership's name remains the same – and so does the Bell family business philosophy that inspired it.

LOU BELL WITH ED SULLIVAN
LOU BELL MOTORS DENVER, CO, 1950'S

COMMUNITY CHEVROLET | 200 WEST OLIVE AVE. BURBANK, CA 91502 | (866) 766-1045 | WWW.YOURCHEVY.COM